LIGUORI CATHOLIC BIBLE STUDY

# Biblical Novellas

## TOBIT, JUDITH, ESTHER, 1 AND 2 MACCABEES

### WILLIAM A. ANDERSON, DMIN, PHD

D0124203

Liguori
LIGUORI, MISSOURI

*Imprimi Potest:*
Harry Grile, CSsR, Provincial
Denver Province, The Redemptorists

Printed with Ecclesiastical Permission and Approved for Private or Instructional Use
*Nihil Obstat:* Rev. Msgr. Kevin Michael Quirk, JCD, JV
        *Censor Librorum*
*Imprimatur:* + Michael J. Bransfield
        Bishop of Wheeling-Charleston [West Virginia]
        March 19, 2014

Published by Liguori Publications
Liguori, Missouri 63057

To order, visit Liguori.org or call 800-325-9521.

**Library of Congress Cataloging-in-Publication Data**

Anderson, William Angor, 1937-
  Biblical novellas : Tobit, Judith, Esther, 1 and 2 Maccabees / William A. Anderson, DMin, PhD.
  pages cm.—(Liguori Catholic Bible study)
  1. Bible. Apocrypha. Tobit—Study and teaching. 2. Bible. Apocrypha. Judith—Study and teaching. 3. Bible. Esther—Study and teaching. 4. Bible. Apocrypha. Maccabees—Study and teaching. 5. Catholic Church—Doctrines. I. Title.
  BS1725.55.A53 2014
  229'.20071—dc23

                    2014018794
p ISBN: 978-0-7648-2138-7
e ISBN: 978-0-7648-6986-0

Liguori Publications, a nonprofit corporation, is an apostolate of The Redemptorists. To learn more about The Redemptorists, visit Redemptorists.com.

Printed in the United States of America
18 17 16 15 14 / 5 4 3 2 1
First Edition

# Contents

> NOTE: The length of each Bible section varies. Group leaders should combine sections as needed to fit the number of sessions in their program.

# Dedication

THIS SERIES is lovingly dedicated to the memory of my parents, Angor and Kathleen Anderson, in gratitude for all they shared with all who knew them, especially my siblings and me.

# Acknowledgments

BIBLE STUDIES and reflections depend on the help of others who read the manuscript and make suggestions. I am especially indebted to Sister Anne Francis Bartus, CSJ, DMin, whose vast experience and knowledge were very helpful in bringing this series to its final form.

# Introduction to
## _Liguori Catholic Bible Study_

READING THE BIBLE can be daunting. It's a complex book, and many a person of goodwill has tried to read the Bible and ended up putting it down in utter confusion. It helps to have a companion, and _Liguori Catholic Bible Study_ is a solid one. Over the course of this series, you'll learn about biblical messages, themes, personalities, and events and understand how the books of the Bible rose out of the need to address new situations.

Across the centuries, people of faith have asked, "Where is God in this moment?" Millions of Catholics look to the Bible for encouragement in their journey of faith. Wisdom teaches us not to undertake Bible study alone, disconnected from the Church that was given Scripture to share and treasure. When used as a source of prayer and thoughtful reflection, the Bible comes alive.

Your choice of a Bible-study program should be dictated by what you want to get out of it. One goal of _Liguori Catholic Bible Study_ is to give readers greater familiarity with the Bible's structure, themes, personalities, and message. But that's not enough. This program will also teach you to use Scripture in your prayer. God's message is as compelling and urgent today as ever, but we get only part of the message when it's memorized and stuck in our head. It's meant for the entire person—physical, emotional, and spiritual.

We're baptized into life with Christ, and we're called to live more fully with Christ today as we practice the values of justice, peace, forgiveness, and community. God's new covenant was written on the hearts of the people of Israel; we, their spiritual descendants, are loved that intimately by God today. _Liguori Catholic Bible Study_ will draw you closer to God, in whose image and likeness we are fashioned.

## Group and Individual Study

The *Liguori Catholic Bible Study* series is intended for group and individual study and prayer. This series gives you the tools to start a study group. Gathering two or three people in a home or announcing the meeting of a Bible-study group in a parish or community can bring surprising results. Each lesson in this series contains a section to help groups study, reflect, pray, and share biblical reflections. Each lesson but the first also has a second section for individual study.

Many people who want to learn more about the Bible don't know where to begin. This series gives them a place to start and helps them continue until they're familiar with all the books of the Bible.

Bible study can be a lifelong project, always enriching those who wish to be faithful to God's Word. When people complete a study of the whole Bible, they can begin again, making new discoveries with each new adventure into the Word of God.

# Lectio Divina
## (Sacred Reading)

BIBLE STUDY isn't just a matter of gaining intellectual knowledge of the Bible; it's also about gaining a greater understanding of God's love and concern for creation. The purpose of reading and knowing the Bible is to enrich our relationship with God. God loves us and gave us the Bible to illustrate that love. In his April 12, 2013, address before the Pontifical Biblical Commission, Pope Francis stressed that "the Church's life and mission are founded on the Word of God which is the soul of theology and at the same time inspires the whole of Christian life."

## The Meaning of *Lectio Divina*

*Lectio divina* is a Latin expression that means "divine or sacred reading." The process for *lectio divina* consists of Scripture readings, reflection, and prayer. Many clergy, religious, and laity use *lectio divina* in their daily spiritual reading to develop a closer and more loving relationship with God. Learning about Scripture has as its purpose the living of its message, which demands a period of reflection on Scripture passages.

## Prayer and *Lectio Divina*

Prayer is a necessary element for the practice of *lectio divina*. The entire process of reading and reflecting is a prayer. It's not merely an intellectual pursuit; it's also a spiritual one. Page 15 includes an Opening Prayer for gathering one's thoughts before moving on to the passages in each section.

This prayer may be used privately or in a group. For those who use the book for daily spiritual reading, the prayer for each section may be repeated each day. Some may wish to keep a journal of each day's meditation.

## Pondering the Word of God

*Lectio divina* is the ancient Christian spiritual practice of reading the holy Scriptures with intentionality and devotion. This practice helps Christians center themselves and descend to the level of the heart to enter an inner quiet space, finding God.

This sacred reading is distinct from reading for knowledge or information, and it's more than the pious practice of spiritual reading. It is the practice of opening ourselves to the action and inspiration of the Holy Spirit. As we intentionally focus on and become present to the inner meaning of the Scripture passage, the Holy Spirit enlightens our mind and heart. We come to the text willing to be influenced by a deeper meaning that lies within the words and thoughts we ponder.

In this space, we open ourselves to be challenged and changed by the inner meaning we experience. We approach the text in a spirit of faith and obedience as a disciple ready to be taught by the Holy Spirit. As we savor the sacred text, we let go of our usual control of how we expect God to act in our life and surrender our heart and conscience to the flow of the divine (*divina*) through the reading (*lectio*).

The fundamental principle of *lectio divina* leads us to understand the profound mystery of the Incarnation, "The Word became flesh," not only in history but also within us.

## Praying *Lectio* Today

Before you begin, relax your body and maintain a posture of prayer (back straight, eyes shut, feet flat on the floor). Then practice these four simple actions:

1. Read a passage from Scripture or the daily Mass readings. This is known as *lectio*. (If the Word of God is read aloud, the hearers listen attentively.)

2. Pray the selected passage with attention as you listen for a specific meaning that comes to mind. Once again, the reading is listened to or silently read and reflected or meditated on. This is known as *meditatio*.

3. The exercise becomes active. Pick a word, sentence, or idea that surfaces from your consideration of the chosen text. Does the reading remind you of a person, place, or experience? If so, pray about it. Compose your thoughts and reflection into a simple word or phrase. This prayer-thought will help you remove distractions during the *lectio*. This exercise is called *oratio*.

4. In silence, with your eyes closed, quiet yourself and become conscious of your breathing. Let your thoughts, feelings, and concerns fade as you consider the selected passage in the previous step (*oratio*). If you're distracted, use your prayer word to help you return to silence. This is *contemplatio*.

This exercise can take as long as you want, but in the context of this Bible study, 10 to 20 minutes should be sufficient.

Many teachers of prayer call contemplation the prayer of resting in God, a prelude to losing oneself in the presence of God. Scripture is transformed in our hearing as we pray and allow our hearts to unite intimately with the Lord. The Word truly takes on flesh, and this time it is manifested in our flesh.

# How to Use This Bible-Study Companion

THE BIBLE, along with the commentaries and reflections found in this study, will help participants become familiar with the Scripture texts and lead them to reflect more deeply on the texts' messages. At the end of this study, participants will have a firm grasp of the Biblical Novellas, becoming therefore more aware of the spiritual nourishment these books offer. This study is not only an intellectual adventure, it's also a spiritual one. The reflections lead participants into their own journey with the Scripture readings.

## Context

When the authors wrote and edited the Biblical Novellas, they were presenting stories about men and women dedicated to the Lord and the Temple. To help readers learn about each passage in relation to those around it, each lesson begins with an overview that puts the Scripture passages into context.

## Part 1: Group Study

To give participants a comprehensive study of Biblical Novellas, this study is divided into seven lessons. Lesson 1 is group study only; Lessons 2 through 7 are divided into Part 1, group study, and Part 2, individual study. For example, Lesson 2 covers the Book of Tobit, chapters 4 through 14. The study group reads and discusses only chapters 4 through 6 (Part 1). Participants privately read and reflect on chapters 7 through 14 (Part 2).

Group study may or may not include *lectio divina*. With *lectio divina*, the group meets for ninety minutes using the first format on page 13. Without *lectio divina*, the group meets for one hour using the format at the bottom of page 13, and participants are urged to privately read the *lectio divina* section at the end of Part 1. It contains additional reflections on the Scripture passages studied during the group session that will take participants even further into the passages.

## Part 2: Individual Study

The passages not covered in Part 1 are divided into shorter components, one to be studied each day. Participants who don't belong to a study group can use the lessons for private sacred reading. They may choose to reflect on one Scripture passage per day, making it possible for a clearer understanding of the Scripture passages used in their *lectio divina* (sacred reading).

## A PROCESS FOR SACRED READING

Liguori Publications has designed this study to be user-friendly and manageable. However, group dynamics and leaders vary. We're not trying to keep the Holy Spirit from working in your midst, thus we suggest you decide beforehand which format works best for your group. If you have limited time, you could study the Bible as a group and save prayer and reflection for personal time.

However, if your group wishes to digest and feast on sacred Scripture through both prayer and study, we recommend you spend closer to ninety minutes each week by gathering to study and pray with Scripture. *Lectio divina* (see page 8) is an ancient contemplative prayer form that moves readers from the head to the heart in meeting the Lord. We strongly suggest using this prayer form whether in individual or group study.

## GROUP-STUDY FORMATS

### 1. Bible Study With *Lectio Divina*

*About ninety minutes of group study*

- ✠ Gathering and opening prayer (3–5 minutes)
- ✠ Read each Scripture passage aloud (5 minutes)
- ✠ Silently review the commentary and prepare to discuss it with the group (3–5 minutes)
- ✠ Discuss the Scripture passage along with the commentary and reflection (30 minutes)
- ✠ Read each Scripture passage aloud a second time, followed by quiet time for meditation and contemplation (5 minutes)
- ✠ Spend some time in prayer with the selected passage. Group participants will slowly read the Scripture passage a third time in silence, listening for the voice of God as they read (10–20 minutes)
- ✠ Shared reflection (10–15 minutes)
- ✠ Closing prayer (3–5 minutes)

*To become acquainted with* lectio divina, *see page 8.*

### 2. Bible Study

*About one hour of group study*

- ✠ Gathering and opening prayer (3–5 minutes)
- ✠ Read each Scripture passage aloud (5 minutes)
- ✠ Silently review the commentary and prepare to discuss it with the group (3–5 minutes)
- ✠ Discuss the Scripture passage along with the commentary and reflection (40 minutes)
- ✠ Closing prayer (3–5 minutes)

## Notes to the Leader

✠ Bring a copy of the *New American Bible,* revised edition.

✠ Plan which sections will be covered each week of your Bible study.

✠ Read the material in advance of each session.

✠ Establish written ground rules. (Example: We won't keep you longer than ninety minutes; don't dominate the sharing by arguing or debating.)

✠ Meet in an appropriate and welcoming gathering space (church building, meeting room, house).

✠ Provide name tags and perhaps use a brief icebreaker for the first meeting; ask participants to introduce themselves.

✠ Mark the Scripture passage(s) that will be read during the session.

✠ Decide how you would like the Scripture to be read aloud (whether by one or multiple readers).

✠ Use a clock or watch.

✠ Provide extra Bibles (or copies of the Scripture passages) for participants who don't bring their Bible.

✠ Ask participants to read the introduction (page 16) before the first session.

✠ Tell participants which passages to study and urge them to read the passages and commentaries before the meeting.

✠ If you opt to use the *lectio divina* format, familiarize yourself with this prayer form ahead of time.

## Notes to the Participants

✠ Bring a copy of the *New American Bible,* revised edition.

✠ Read the introduction (page 16) before the first session.

✠ Read the Scripture passages and commentaries before each session.

✠ Be prepared to share and listen respectfully. (This is not a time to debate beliefs or argue.)

## Opening Prayer

*Leader:*  O God, come to my assistance.

*Response:*  O Lord, make haste to help me.

*Leader:*  Glory be to the Father, and to the Son, and to the Holy Spirit...

*Response:*  ...as it was in the beginning, is now, and ever shall be, world without end. Amen.

*Leader:*  Christ is the vine and we are the branches. As branches linked to Jesus, the vine, we are called to recognize that the Scriptures are always being fulfilled in our lives. It is the living Word of God living on in us. Come, Holy Spirit, fill the hearts of your faithful and kindle in us the fire of your divine wisdom, knowledge, and love.

*Response:*  Open our minds and hearts as we study your great love for us as shown in the Bible.

*Reader:*  (Open your Bible to the assigned Scripture(s) and read in a paced, deliberate manner. Pause for one minute, listening for a word, phrase, or image that you may use in your *lectio divina* practice.)

## Closing Prayer

*Leader:*  Let us pray as Jesus taught us.

*Response:*  Our Father...

*Leader:*  Lord, inspire us with your Spirit as we study your Word in the Bible. Be with us this day and every day as we strive to know you and serve you and to love as you love. We believe that through your goodness and love, the Spirit of the Lord is truly upon us. Allow the words of the Bible, your Word, to capture us and inspire us to live as you live and to love as you love.

*Response:*  Amen.

*Leader:*  May the divine assistance remain with us always.

*Response:*  In the name of the Father, and of the Son, and of the Holy Spirit. Amen.

## INTRODUCTION

# Biblical Novellas

## TOBIT, JUDITH, ESTHER,

## 1 AND 2 MACCABEES

Biblical Novellas have as their purpose to instruct, encourage, and entertain. They tell interesting stories about the activity of God in the lives of people, helping them in times of crisis, and calling them to courageous acts of faith. Biblical Novellas in this text contain the stories found in the books of Tobit, Judith, Esther, and 1 and 2 Maccabees. The books were written long after the Israelites returned from their Babylonian exile. Further details about each book will be found in the context of each chapter.

# The Book of Tobit (I)

## TOBIT 1—3

*"You are righteous, Lord, and all your deeds are just; All your ways are mercy and fidelity; you are judge of the world" (3:2).*

**Opening Prayer** (SEE PAGE 15)

## Context

The Book of Tobit is a fictitious story named after Tobit, the leading character in the book. He is a devout Israelite living in exile in Nineveh around 722 BC who suffered despite his faithfulness to the Lord. The book, written to instruct and edify its audience, was most likely written between 200 and 180 BC by an unknown author. Historical inaccuracies in the book point to an author who is looking back through distant history as he structures his story.

The first three chapters introduce an Israelite who is faithful to Mosaic Law, going to great lengths to continue worshiping in the Temple in Jerusalem. He helps the poor, the orphan, the widow, and the alien, and he buries his dead kinfolk. He has a wife named Anna and a son named Tobiah. The book introduces the story of Sarah, a woman who attempted marriage seven times and whose husbands died on their wedding night.

## GROUP STUDY (TOBIT 1—3)

Read aloud Tobit 1—3.

### *1—2:8 Tobit's Ordeal*

The introduction to the Book of Tobit is a superscript detailing some background about Tobit. "Tobit" means "God is my welfare." Since Tobit was writing after the return of the people of Judah from exile, during the period of the second Temple built in Jerusalem, the genealogy of a person had become important, showing a person's link with ancient Israelites. The names of Tobit's ancestors end with the suffix "el," which means "God." Tobit names his father Tobiel and offers the names of six other generations previous to his father.

Tobit belonged to the tribe of Naphtali, named after one of the twelve sons of Jacob. The names given in the narrative as being in the territory of Naphtali are unidentified towns of Galilee. The story about Tobit takes place during the days of Shalmaneser, the king of the Assyrians (727–722 BC). Shalmaneser took Tobit into exile in Assyria with the people of Naphtali in 722.

In verse 3, Tobit begins to tell his own story, claiming he was always faithful and righteous in the sight of the Lord. He performed a number of acts of charity for his kindred and his people, who marched into captivity to Nineveh, the capital of Assyria.

Tobit describes his former life before his captivity. Jeroboam, an administrator under King Solomon, led a revolt against a son of Solomon and, along with ten tribes of the Israelites, formed the northern kingdom of Israel. Tobit belonged to the northern kingdom. Jeroboam saw his people returning to the Temple in Jerusalem, the city of David, for the major Israelite feasts and realized he would have difficulty controlling his kingdom if the people of the north kept returning to the south for these feasts.

Jeroboam established sanctuaries in Dan and Bethel for the people of the north to offer sacrifice without having to go to Jerusalem. He placed golden calves in the sanctuary as thrones for the God of Israel. In time, the people forgot about the calves being the thrones for God and began to worship the calves as gods. While Tobit's kindred from Naphtali would go to Dan to worship the golden calf, he would go to Jerusalem for the festivals as decreed by the Book of Deuteronomy: "...to the place which the Lord, your God, chooses as the dwelling place for his name you shall bring all that I command you: your burnt offerings and sacrifices, your tithes and personal contributions, and every special offering you have vowed to the Lord" (12:11).

Tobit brought to Jerusalem the first fruits of the crops, the firstlings of the flock, the tithes of the livestock, and the first shearing of sheep and presented them to the priests, the sons of Aaron, at the altar. He also offered tithes of grain, wine, olive oil, pomegranates, figs, and other fruits. Each year, Tobit would give a second tithe in money, and in the third year he would tithe to orphans, widows, and converts who joined the Israelites. He did this in obedience to the Law of Moses, as he was taught by his paternal grandmother.

Unlike many of the exiles who married foreign women, Tobit married a woman named Anna, who belonged to his ancestral family. They had a son whom they named Tobiah. Since Tobit refused to eat the food of the Gentiles, as many of his kindred did, the Lord rewarded him by granting him favor with Shalmaneser who made him a purchasing agent for all the king's needs. Until the death of Shalmaneser, he would travel to Media, the land of the Medes, to buy provisions for him. Years earlier, when the Assyrians invaded the northern kingdom, they sent some of the Israelites into exile in the land of the Medes so Tobit would visit some of his kindred in that country. This gave him the opportunity to deposit pouches of silver worth thousands of dollars in trust with his kinsman Gabael, who lived in the land of Media.

After the death of Shalmaneser, who was followed by Sennacherib, Tobit no longer traveled to Media due to rising dangers for travelers. Sennacherib (705–681 BC) was actually the son of Sargon II, not the son of Shalmaneser.

Tobit continued to help his kindred while Shalmaneser was king. He would share his bread with them and bring them clothing. When he found some of his people who had died and were cast outside Nineveh without being buried, he would bury them. Sennacherib camped near Judah and was preparing to invade the kingdom of Judah, but the night before he planned to invade, an angel of the Lord killed 185,000 men of the Assyrian army (2 Kings 19:35–36). Sennacherib had to flee back to Nineveh. In his rage, he killed many Israelites in Nineveh. Tobit secretly buried the bodies out of respect for his people.

When Sennacherib later looked for the bodies which were apparently meant to remain visible as a lesson of the Assyrian retaliation, he could not find them. One of the citizens of Nineveh informed the king about Tobit burying the bodies, and Tobit had to flee for his life. Everything he owned in Nineveh was confiscated and taken to the king's palace. The only ones remaining at home were his wife, Anna, and their son, Tobiah.

Forty days later, two of the king's sons assassinated him and fled the country. Esarhaddon became king (681–669 BC). The new king placed a man named Ahiqar in charge of the administration of the kingdom. Ahiqar had previously been the chief cupbearer, keeper of the signet ring, and treasury accountant under Sennacherib. Esarhaddon reappointed him to these high offices. Ahiqar was actually a legendary character whom the author of the Book of Tobit chose to name as a relative of Tobit. According to the story, Ahiqar interceded for him, enabling Tobit to return to his wife and son.

"The Story of the Wisdom of Ahiqar" was a very popular legend in ancient times. According to the story, Ahiqar was chancellor under Sennacherib, king of Assyria. When Sennacherib was killed, his son, King Esarhaddon, became king and put Ahiqar in charge of the entire administration of the kingdom. Ahiqar adopted his nephew, Nadin, and trained him to become his successor, but Nadin, once in power, plotted to have Ahiqar killed. In some translations, "Ahiqar" is translated as "Ahikar" and "Nadin" is translated as "Nadab." Ahiqar was able to escape and hide in a cave.

One day, the king wanted some riddles explained, but Nadin was unable to solve them. When the king regretted the loss of Ahiqar, Ahiqar's chosen executioner disclosed Ahiqar's escape. The king sent for Ahiqar, who solved the riddles. When Nadin's plot was discovered, he was scourged and thrown into a dungeon where he died. The author of Tobit may have chosen the name of Ahiqar to show a parallel between Ahiqar's story and that of Tobit's.

At home with his wife and son, Tobit was about to celebrate the spring harvest feast of Pentecost with a fine dinner. According to Deuteronomy 16:14, the festival is celebrated with one's family and slaves, along with the resident alien, orphans, and widows. Being a righteous man, Tobit did not eat before sending Tobiah out to bring in whatever worshiper of God he could find among their poor and needy kindred.

Tobiah went out, but he soon returned, crying out that he has found a murdered Israelite in the marketplace. Leaving the dinner untouched, Tobit rushed out and carried the body into a room so he could bury it at sundown. The room may have been in the home of the dead person. He returned to his own home, washed, and ate his meal in sorrow and mourning. After touching a dead body, a true Israelite had to perform a ritual washing. Tobit recalled an oracle of Amos that said: "I will turn your feasts into mourning and all your songs into dirges" (Amos 8:10). At sunset, as he buried the body, his neighbors ridiculed him for burying the dead, a deed that had forced him to flee in fear in the past.

### 2:9—3:6 Tobit's Blindness

Tobit again performed his ritual washing and lay down against the wall in his courtyard. Since he had already gone home and eaten after he carried the corpse to a room, it is not clear why he laid down outside his home at this point. The droppings from sparrows on the top of the wall fell into his eyes, causing blindness. People of ancient times described blindness as white scales on the eyes. The more Tobit went to doctors for a cure, the more blind he became, until he was totally blind. He lived with this condition for four years. Ahiqar cared for him for two years until Ahiqar left for the land of Elam.

Anna performed the woman's work of weaving cloth to support them. One day, her employers paid the correct wages and added a goat for a meal. When Tobit heard the goat bleating, he accused his wife of stealing it and ordered her to give it back to its owners. Tobit still refused to believe her when she said the employers gave her the goat as a bonus. Tobit became angry with her. She retorted by asking Tobit where his charitable deeds and righteous acts were now, saying everyone knows what happened to him. Anna's words are similar to those of Job's wife, who asks Job where his innocence is now that he is suffering. Both women are asking the same question central to both books. If God blesses a person for being righteous, why are the righteous punished?

Tobit declares he broke down in tears at this rebuke and prayed, praising God for being righteous and performing just deeds. He declared the Lord is merciful and faithful, a just judge of the world. He begged the Lord to look on him with favor and not to punish him for his inadvertent sins or those of his ancestors. In ancient times, people believed the sins of an ancestor brought punishment to their offspring. Tobit notes the Lord abandoned his ancestors for their disobedience, allowing them to be plundered, captured, and killed. He believed the Lord's judgments on him and his ancestors were deserved, and he pleaded with the Lord to allow him to die rather than live. Like Tobit, Jonah also protested it was better for him to die than to live (see Jonah 4:3). When he buried the dead, Tobit suffered the taunts of his neighbors. He begged for death, saying it is better to die than to endure so much grief and such reproaches.

### 3:7–17 Sarah's Plight

On the day Tobit prayed to die, an event that would affect his family's life was taking place in Ecbatana, which is Hamadan in current-day Iran. From this point on, the story shifts from being told in the first person to the third person. Sarah, a daughter of Raguel, is enduring reproaches from one of her father's maids. "Raguel" means "friend of God." Sarah's father had given her to seven husbands, but a wicked demon, known as a "demon of wrath," killed each one of them before they could have intercourse with her. A maid accused her of killing her husbands, saying she had been given in marriage to seven men without bearing the name of any one of them. According to the maid, Sarah beat her and other maids. She tells Sarah to join her husbands in death, hoping never to see a son or daughter from Sarah.

Sarah becomes so despondent, she contemplates hanging herself, but she fears people would reproach her father, who would then die from deep sorrow. She believes it would be better to beg the Lord to let her die and no longer have to endure these reproaches. With hands outstretched, she would pray toward the window facing Jerusalem, as was the custom.

Sarah begs the Lord to help her avoid reproaches by taking her life. Just as Job declared his innocence in the midst of his suffering, Sarah declares she was clean of any defilement with a man and has never shamed her name or her father's name. Since she has no brothers or sisters and no kinsman or close relative left to marry, she asks why she should live any longer. Sarah is unaware Tobiah exists. She prays that if the Lord does not wish to take her life, then to look upon her with favor and pity so she will never again have to endure reproaches.

God hears the prayer of Tobit and Sarah at the same time and sends the angel Raphael to eventually heal them both, blessing Tobit with sight and giving Sarah as a wife to Tobiah and ridding her of the monster, Asmodeus. "Raphael" means "God has healed." It is Tobiah's lot, as a relative of Sarah's, to have the next right to marry her. At that moment, Tobit turns from his courtyard and Sarah comes down from the upstairs room.

## Review Questions

1. What gave Tobit the courage to act as such a righteous person?
2. Why did God punish Tobit?
3. What do the early chapters of the Book of Tobit tell us about prayer?
4. Is it better to die rather than face suffering, ridicule, or rejection?

---

### Closing Prayer (SEE PAGE 15)

Pray the closing prayer now or after *lectio divina*.

---

### Lectio Divina (SEE PAGE 8)

Relax your body and maintain a posture of prayer (back straight, eyes shut, feet flat on the floor). This exercise can take as long as you want, but in the context of this Bible study, 10 to 20 minutes should be sufficient.

The meditations that follow are provided only to help group participants use this prayer form, but note that *lectio* is intended to bring one to a place of prayerful contemplation where the Word of God speaks to the hearer from his or her heart. (See page 8 for further instruction.)

### Tobit's Ordeal (1—2:8)

In the 1924 Olympics, Eric Liddell, a Scottish runner and missionary in China, won the 400-meter race for the British, but he almost missed the competition because he refused to run on a Sunday. Despite pressure from the prince of Wales and the British Olympic Committee, Liddell still refused to compete. A teammate allowed Liddell to run in his place in a 400-meter race held on a Thursday. An American Olympic Team masseur expressed his admiration for Liddell for remaining true to his convictions. In many ways, Liddell was like Tobit, who remained faithful to his Jewish convictions, no matter how challenging and foolish his dedication seemed.

✠ *What can I learn from this passage?*

### Tobit's Blindness (2:9—3:6)

A question many good people have been asking throughout the ages is, "Why do bad things happen to good people?" The Book of Job and the Book of Tobit ask the same question. Job and Tobit are good people, yet they suffered. The answer in most books of the Bible is the Lord tests people to determine if they will remain faithful in times of disappointment or turmoil. The fact is God allows suffering, but God is not the direct cause of suffering. Good people survive bad things and remain faithful to the Lord.

✠ *What can I learn from this passage?*

### Sarah's Plight (3:7–17)

Sarah and Tobit suffered a great deal, but they still prayed and trusted in God. Some people have minor problems in life and abandon God or their faith, while others endure overwhelming difficulties and still remain faithful. Paul the Apostle wrote, "What will separate us from the love of Christ? Will anguish, or distress, or persecution, or famine, or nakedness, or peril, or the sword" (Romans 8:35)? He answers his own question when he writes, "No, in all these things we conquer overwhelmingly through him who loved us" (Romans 8:37). We all hope to have the trust and dedication of Paul in times of turmoil.

✠ *What can I learn from this passage?*

# The Book of Tobit (II)

## TOBIT 4–14

*It is better to give alms than to store up gold, for almsgiving saves from death, and purges all sin (12:8–9).*

**Opening Prayer** (SEE PAGE 15)

## Context

**Part 1: Tobit 4—6** Tobiah prepares to travel to Media to receive the money his father left with Gabael. He chooses Raphael as his guide, not knowing Raphael was an angel. Raphael plans to bring Tobiah to the home of Raguel, who has a daughter named Sarah. His intention is for Tobiah to marry Sarah.

**Part 2: Tobit 7—14** Raphael helps Tobiah free Sarah from the grip of a demon and Tobiah marries her. When Tobiah returns home with his new wife, Raphael helps him cure Tobit's blindness. Raphael reveals his true identity. When Tobit is dying, he tells his son to flee from Nineveh after his death and the death of his mother. Tobiah does as his father commands, and Nineveh and Assyria fall into the hands of the king of Media.

# PART 1: GROUP STUDY (TOBIT 4—6)

Read aloud Tobit 4—6.

### 4 Preparation for the Journey

Calling Tobiah to him, Tobit decides it was time to tell his son about the money he left with Gabael. He first instructs Tobiah with maxims similar to those found in Proverbs and Sirach. His first concern is a proper burial. Since Tobit showed such concern for the dead, it would be natural for him to be concerned about his own burial.

Tobit instructs Tobiah to honor his mother, never abandoning her and doing all that pleases her. These instructions were already contained in the Ten Commandments given to Moses, holding a place of honor immediately after the first three commandments concerning one's relationship with God (see Exodus 20:12). Tobit reminds Tobiah of the dangers encountered by his mother when he was in her womb. Many women in Tobit's era did not survive the birth of a child. Tobit instructed his son to bury his mother with him (Tobit) in the same grave.

Tobit instructs his son in living a righteous life. He must remain faithful to the Lord and to the commandments, avoiding the ways of the wicked. Although Tobit himself lived a righteous life and had to endure suffering, he tells Tobiah those who live righteously will prosper in all they do.

Tobit instructs Tobiah to give alms and not to neglect the poor. Otherwise, the Lord will not look on him favorably. Whether he has much or little, he should give alms out of the abundance or little he has. In doing this, he will be storing up a treasure for himself as a help on the day of hardship. Giving alms will deliver Tobiah from death and from entering into Darkness, meaning the place of the dead. Tobit is not saying Tobiah will not die, but he is saying Tobiah will live a long life if he gives alms because the Most High looks upon this as a praiseworthy deed.

Tobit warns Tobiah to guard himself against fornication, and even more so, not to marry a foreign woman, a woman not of his father's tribe. Although many of the Israelites married foreign women while in exile, marrying within the ancestral family was believed to be important in the eyes of God.

He reminds Tobiah his family comes from a line of prophets, namely Noah, Abraham, Isaac, and Jacob who married within their own kindred and who were blessed with children whose posterity would inherit the Promised Land. Tobiah is to love his kindred and not to act arrogantly by refusing to take a wife from among them. Choosing a wife outside their kindred would appear to snub their kindred's women. Such arrogance would lead to ruin and instability. The one who marries outside one's kindred would find himself rejected by his relatives and in an unstable relationship with a foreign woman.

Tobit offers a list of concise instructions for living righteously. Since idleness leads to poverty and famine, Tobiah should guard against being idle. He should not withhold overnight the wages of those who worked for him. If he serves God, he will receive a great reward. He must be wise in all he does and says. He must not do to another what he himself hates. He must not drink wine to the point of being drunk and becoming known as a drunkard.

Care for the poor and needy was an important part of the Lord's message for the Israelites. Tobit instructs Tobiah to give some of his food to the hungry and clothing to the naked, even to the point of giving over whatever he has left. He tells Tobiah to pour out his wine on the grave of the righteous, not the wicked. This means a person should provide for the family of a faithful deceased person.

Tobit urges Tobiah to seek counsel from every wise person and not to treat it lightly. He should always praise the Lord and beg the Lord for guidance and help so all his endeavors and plans may prosper. Because the Israelites have faith in the one true Lord, they possess wise counsel from the Lord, something other nations do not have. Whomever the Lord wishes to raise up or cast down rises or falls as the Lord wishes. Tobit ends his instructions, exhorting Tobiah to never abandon these commands.

Tobit informs Tobiah about the money he deposited with Gabael, saying not to fear, even though they themselves live in poverty. He says Tobiah will possess great wealth as long as he fears the Lord, avoids sin, and does what is right before the Lord.

## 5 The Angel Raphael

Tobiah obediently tells his father he will do all his father commands. Since he does not know Gabael and Gabael does not know him, Tobiah asks what sign he can give to Gabael so Gabael will trust him with the money. He adds he does not know the way to Media.

Tobit states Gabael gave him his bond and he gave Gabael his. A bond was a document which was cut in two, with each party keeping a half. Tobit put one part with the money he left in Gabael's keeping. That was twenty years ago. Tobit advises Tobiah to find a trustworthy person to make the journey with him, and when they return, he will pay his companion's wages. He urges Tobiah to bring back the money while Tobit is still alive.

Tobiah goes out and sees the angel Raphael standing before him, although he does not know Raphael is an angel of the Lord. In many folklore stories, angels often appear in the story without informing people they are in the presence of an angel. When Tobiah asks Raphael where he came from, Raphael answers he is an Israelite, one of Tobiah's kindred who came there to work. Tobiah asks if he knows the way to Media, and Raphael replies he knows the place well and has traveled all the routes many times. He adds he used to stay with their kinsman, Gabael. Raphael says it is a good two days' journey from Ecbatana to Rages. In reality, it is about 180 miles between the two cities, and it would ordinarily take more than two days.

After relating to Raphael he will pay his wages, Tobiah goes to his father and informs him about finding a fellow Israelite who will travel with him to Media. Tobit instructs him to summon the man so he may inquire about his family and tribe and discern whether he is trustworthy enough as a traveling companion for his son. Tobiah brings Raphael into the house, and Raphael greets Tobit with the words, "Joyful greetings to you." This allows Tobit to declare he has no joy left since he is blind, like the dead who no longer see the light. This passage allows the author to remind the reader of Tobit's blindness. Tobit declares he can hear voices but not see the speakers. Raphael tells him to be courageous, God's healing is near.

Tobit tells Raphael he will pay his wages if he will go to Media with his son. Raphael agrees to go with Tobiah, reiterating he knows all the routes since he has traveled to Media many times before. He states he has crossed the plains of Ecbatana and knows the mountains in which Rages is situated. In reality, Ecbatana is in mountains which are higher than the mountains in which Rages is situated. This adds to the inconsistencies found in the narrative.

Tobit asks Raphael about his family and tribe. The angel feigns surprise, asking why Tobit wants to know his tribe as long as he is a hired hand ready to travel. Tobit pushes for an answer to his question and Raphael replies, "I am Azariah, son of the great Hananiah, one of your own kindred"(5:13). The name "Azariah" means "God has helped," and Hananiah means "God has shown mercy." Tobit welcomes him and begs him not to be angry with him for wanting to know the truth about his family.

Tobit agrees Raphael is indeed a kinsman from a good and noble family. Tobit says, "I knew Hananiah and Nathan, the two sons of the great Shemeliah" (5:14). Nathan means "God has given," and Shemeliah means "God has heard." Tobit says he used to go to Jerusalem with them, where they would worship together. The text proves Tobit was not the only Israelite of the northern kingdom who dared to go to Jerusalem for major feasts. Tobit tells Raphael he comes from good lineage, and welcomes him.

Tobit promises to give him a drachma as his wages, which is equivalent to seventeen cents a day, a normal day's wage, and he will pay the expenses for him and his son. He promises to add a bonus. Raphael agrees to go with Tobiah, telling Tobit not to fear. He states the way is safe and they will return in good health. Tobit blesses Raphael and bids his son to prepare for the journey and leave with his kinsman. He prays God will protect them and keep them safe on their journey and on their way back. Still unaware Raphael is an angel, he prays the Lord's angel will accompany them for their safety.

Tobiah kisses his father and mother and leaves. Anna, his mother, asked Tobit why he sent his son away. She urges him to forgo his money in exchange for their child, adding the Lord provided them with enough. Tobit reassures her she will see their son return in good health. Believing a good angel will journey with him, he states the journey will be successful and he will return in good health. This assurance ended her weeping.

## 6 Tobiah's Journey to Media

The author speaks of a dog, apparently belonging to the family, following Tobiah and the angel. This mention of a domestic animal in the story is unique and a homey addition. On the first night, they camp beside the Tigris River. The Tigris is actually west of Nineveh and would most likely not have been the route one would take to Media. This misdirection is another inconsistency found in the story.

When Tobiah goes to wash his feet in the Tigris, a large fish leaps up and tries to swallow his foot. Tobias shouts out, and Raphael calls to him to seize and hold the fish, which he did. The angel instructs Tobiah to cut the fish open and take its gall, heart, and liver with him. The ancients used the gall, heart, and liver of a fish for medicinal purposes. Tobiah then roasts and eats other parts of the fish, salting the remainder for the journey. There is no mention of Raphael eating the fish.

As they neared Media, Tobiah asks Raphael about using the heart, liver, and gall of the fish as medicine. Raphael explains burning the fish's heart and liver would produce smoke to drive an evil spirit away from a man or woman who is afflicted by a demon. The demon would never return. If a person applies the gall to the eyes of one who has white scales and blows into the eyes, the blind person's sight will return.

As they neared Ecbatana, Raphael reveals his real purpose for traveling with Tobiah. He declares that night they will stay at the house of Raguel, who has an only child, a beautiful daughter named Sarah. Since Tobiah is her closest relative, he has first right to marry her. He will also have the right to inherit her father's estate. According to Israelite law, a woman without brothers must marry within the clan of her ancestral tribe. In doing this, the one she marries has a right to her father's estate, thus keeping the estate from passing on to another Israelite tribe (see Numbers 36:6–9).

Raphael praises Sarah, saying she is the daughter of a good man and is wise, courageous, and beautiful. He intends to speak to Raguel that night so Tobiah can take Sarah as his bride. Since Raguel knows Tobiah has first right to marry his daughter, Raguel cannot refuse. Raphael declares Tobiah will take her back with him to his house. Tobiah, who had no say in the matter up to this point, tells Raphael he heard seven husbands of Sarah died on their wedding night when they approached her. He heard a demon, who was in love with Sarah, caused these deaths. Since the death of the only son of his parents would bring them to their death in sorrow over his loss, Tobiah reveals his fear of the demon.

Raphael reminds Tobiah his father commanded him to marry a woman from his own ancestral tribe. Assuring Tobiah Sarah would be given to him that night as his wife, he urges Tobiah to have no fear. To ward off the demon, Raphael instructs Tobiah to place the fish's liver and heart on the embers intended for incense, and when the demon smells the odor, it will flee and never again approach her. Before Tobiah has intercourse with Sarah, both must first pray to the Lord for mercy and protection. Raphael again tells Tobiah not to fear, since Sarah was set apart for him before the creation of the world. He assumes they will have children who will become like brothers to him. When Tobiah heard all this, he loved her deeply and set his heart on marrying her.

## Review Questions

1. List some of the good deeds Tobit tells Tobiah to practice that are echoed in the life of Jesus.
2. Why did God send Raphael to Tobit and Tobiah?
3. How does Raphael help Tobiah?

---

**Closing Prayer** (SEE PAGE 15)

Pray the closing prayer now or after *lectio divina*.

---

**Lectio Divina** (SEE PAGE 8)

Relax your body and maintain a posture of prayer (back straight, eyes shut, feet flat on the floor). This exercise can take as long as you want, but in the context of this Bible study, 10 to 20 minutes should be sufficient.

The meditations that follow are provided only to help group participants use this prayer form, but note that *lectio* is intended to bring one to a place of prayerful contemplation where the Word of God speaks to the hearer from his or her heart. (See page 8 for further instruction.)

---

### *Preparation for the Journey (4)*

When people prepare for a journey, they usually have their itinerary planned, clothes packed, finances secure, and all the necessary tasks taken care of before leaving. Tobit is not just preparing Tobiah for a trip to Gabael, but for his life journey. He instructs Tobiah how to live a life faithful to the Lord and one that helps others. When we make trips, we very often have roundtrip plans. There is no roundtrip in life. Tobit is giving Tobiah foundation plans, not a roundtrip ticket to life.

✠ *What can I learn from this passage?*

### *The Angel Raphael (5)*

When Tobiah is about to make his trip, the Lord sends an angel as his companion. In our daily life, the Lord sends people who are really angels in our life. They are ordinary people who encourage, support, and sometimes cajole us into becoming a good person. Many of us are angels for others on their journey without us realizing it. God still sends angels, and they are the good people in our life who have a positive influence on our development.

✠ *What can I learn from this passage?*

### *Tobiah's Journey to Media (6)*

The author states the Lord chose Sarah as Tobiah's wife before the world existed. The text makes it sound as though the Lord is directing everything in our life, leaving no room for free will. How much God intervenes directly in our life is a mystery, but theologians tell us God guides us but never forces us to act in a particular manner. When we pray, God inspires us, protects us, gives us courage and opportunities, and responds to our needs, but the final choice of accepting or rejecting God's grace is up to us.

✠ *What can I learn from this passage?*

## PART 2: INDIVIDUAL STUDY (TOBIT 7—14)

### Day 1: Marriage and Healing of Sarah (7—9)

When they arrived at Ecbatana, Tobiah addresses Raphael as Azariah and bids him to take him straight to the house of Raguel. When they arrived at the house of Raguel, they greet him first and he returns the greeting, welcoming them in peace and bringing them into his house. All these are gestures of hospitality.

Raguel exclaims to his wife, Edna, how this young man resembles Tobit, whom he identifies as the son of his uncle. When Edna asks where they have come from, they respond they are descendants of Naphtali who are now captives of Nineveh. She asks if they know their kinsman, Tobit. They answer they know him well. Tobiah tells her Tobit is alive and well and is his father. Upon hearing this, Raguel leaps up, kisses him, and weeps. He blesses Tobiah and declares he is the son of a good and noble father. Although Raguel seems surprised at the presence of Tobit's son, he already knows about Tobit's blindness and declares it to be such a misfortune. Raguel, Edna, and their daughter Sarah begin to weep.

Like Abraham, who greeted three visitors who were angels and prepared a meal for them (see Genesis 18:1–8), Raguel slaughters a ram from the flock for his unexpected guests. After they washed, bathed, and reclined to eat and drink, Tobiah tells Raphael to ask Raguel to give him his kinswoman Sarah in marriage. Raguel overhears Tobiah and urges him to eat and drink, for he has the right to Sarah and Raguel could not refuse it. Raguel admits he previously gave her to seven husbands who were kinsmen and all died on the night they approached her. Raguel tells Tobiah to eat and drink, but Tobiah said he would not eat or drink anything until they settled the matter.

Raguel had to agree to the marriage, as commanded "by the Book of Moses" (7:11), declaring it was already decided in heaven. He said Tobiah and Sarah were now considered a brother and sister, a common expression used for spouses, and he prays the Lord would prosper them both. Raguel calls his daughter and gives her to Tobiah, telling Tobiah to take her as his wife according to the Law of Moses and to bring her safely to his father. Calling to

Edna for writing material, he composes a marriage contract, giving Sarah to Tobiah as his wife in accord with the Law of Moses. He places his seal on it.

Afterward, they eat and drink. Raguel tells his wife to prepare the other bedroom for Sarah. After Edna makes the bed in the room, she brings Sarah there, and weeping, told Sarah to have courage. Although the tears could be tears of joy, they appear to be tears for Tobiah, who will meet with tragedy that night and bring sorrow to Sarah. Sarah's mother prays the Lord will grant her joy and not grief.

In chapter 8, Sarah's parents lead Tobiah to the bedroom. Following Raphael's directions, Tobiah puts the fish's liver and heart on the embers intended for incense. The odor of the fish repulses the demon and it flees to the upper regions of Egypt, a symbolic retreat to the wilderness where demons were said to dwell. Raphael pursues the demon and binds it hand and foot so it cannot return. Raphael returns at once.

When Sarah's parents leave Tobiah and Sarah, Tobiah bids Sarah to pray with him to beg the Lord for mercy and protection. He begins his prayer by praising God as the God of their ancestors and imploring the heavens and all creation to bless the Lord forever. Recalling the story of human creation from the Book of Genesis, he recalls the Lord made Adam and his wife Eve to be his helper and support, and from these two the human race came. In his prayer, he declares the Lord, who saw it was not good for the man to be alone, made a helper to be like himself (see Genesis 2:21–24). Tobiah proclaims he does not take Sarah as his wife out of lust, but with faithfulness. He prays for the Lord to send down mercy on him and her, granting that they will grow old together and be blessed with many children. Together they said, "Amen, amen!" and went to bed for the night.

An amusing interlude takes place as Raguel, fearing Tobiah would die and he (Raguel) would be the laughingstock among the people, digs a grave with the help of his servants. When he finishes, he tells his wife to send one of her maids to see if Tobiah is still alive. If he died, he wants to bury him without anyone knowing about it. The maid finds Tobiah and Sarah sleeping together. The family and servants then praise the Lord for making them happy. Raguel prays, saying what he feared did not happen. He sends his servants out to fill in the grave before anyone knows about it.

Raguel tells Edna to bake many loaves of bread, and he brings two steers and four rams and orders his servants to slaughter them and prepare for the feast. He tells Tobiah he must stay with them for fourteen days, eating and drinking with them for bringing joy to his daughter's afflicted spirit. The usual period of wedding celebrations was seven days, but Tobiah's survival makes everyone doubly happy. Tobiah's family will later celebrate the wedding feast for the usual seven days.

When Raguel sends Tobiah on his journey home, he promises to give him half of what he has and tells him the other half will be his when he and his wife die. With the bond of marriage comes a family bond with Tobiah and the family of Sarah. Raguel declares he is Tobiah's father and Edna is his mother, now and forever.

In chapter 9, Tobiah sends Raphael (Azariah), four servants, and two camels to Gabael to give him the bond, receive the money, and bring him along to the wedding celebration. He knows his father will be conscious of his time away, and if he delays even a single day, it would cause his father great grief. Raphael, with the four servants and two camels, goes to Gabael's house, stays with him, gives him the bond, and informs him about the invitation to the wedding celebration. Gabael counts out the moneybags with the seals, packs them on the camels, and early the next morning travels to the wedding celebration.

Upon entering Raguel's house, they find Tobiah reclining at table. He leaps up and greets Gabael who weeps and blesses him, addressing him as a good and noble child, a son of a righteous and charitable man. He prays the Lord will bless Tobiah, his wife Sarah, and her parents. He praises God for allowing him to witness the very image of Tobit in his son, Tobiah.

### Lectio Divina

Spend 8 to 10 minutes in silent contemplation of the following passage:

Tobiah's prayer on his wedding night is often used as a first reading at weddings. Unfortunately, the Sacramentary for weddings leaves out a very important part of the prayer. It occurs at the end of the prayer when the author writes, "They said together, 'Amen, amen!'"

Although it is not in the Sacramentary, many add this vital ending to show both are one in praying together. Spouses who pray together often find themselves blessed by God.

✠ *What can I learn from this passage?*

## Day 2: The Healing of Tobit (10—11)

The scene shifts back to the anxious parents of Tobiah, who fear for the life of their son when he did not appear as expected. Tobit, although apprehensive, is a bit more optimistic than his wife. He wonders if Tobiah has been detained or if Gabael has died and there is no one to give him the money. Believing Tobiah has died, Tobit's wife weeps and wails over her son. Tobit tries to comfort his wife, telling her not to worry, saying Tobiah is safe and is probably detained in taking care of some business. He believes the kinsman traveling with Tobiah is trustworthy. Anna becomes angry with Tobit, telling him to be still and not try to deceive her into thinking Tobiah is alive. Each day, she would rush out to watch the road taken by her son. She ate nothing. After sunset, she would return home and wail and weep throughout the night, never sleeping.

In the meanwhile, the fourteen days of celebration for the marriage ended, and Tobiah begs Raguel to send him home since his parents must believe they will never see him again. Raguel begs Tobiah to remain with him, saying he would send messengers to his father to give him news about Tobiah. Tobiah insists he be sent back to his father.

Raguel hands over to Tobiah his wife, Sarah, and half of his property: male and female slaves, oxen and sheep, donkeys and camels, clothing, money, and household goods. Embracing Tobiah, he bids him farewell and a safe journey. He prays the Lord of heaven will grant prosperity to him and his wife and prays to see Tobiah's children before he dies. He tells Sarah to honor her father-in-law and mother-in-law, because they are now as much related as the parents who gave her birth. Wishing his daughter peace, he tells her he wants to hear a good report about her as long as he lives.

Edna, addressing Tobiah, prays the Lord will bring him back safely. She, like her husband, hopes to live long enough to see grandchildren. She entrusts her daughter to Tobiah, telling him never to cause her grief. She reminds Tobiah she is now his mother and Sarah is his sister, and she prays they will all prosper. She kisses them both and sets them safely on their trip.

Tobiah leaves filled with joy and blessing the Lord of heaven and earth for making his journey so successful. Blessing Raguel and Edna, he professes he has been commanded by the Lord to honor them all the days of his life.

In chapter 11, as the travelers near a town named Kaserin, opposite Nineveh, Raphael urges Tobiah to rush on ahead of his wife to prepare the house. As Raphael and Tobiah rush ahead, Raphael tells Tobiah to take the gall in his hand. The faithful dog ran along behind them.

When Anna, who was watching the road, saw Tobiah coming, she shouted to Tobit to tell him his son and the man who traveled with him were coming. Before Tobiah came to his father, Raphael instructed him to apply the gall to his father's eyes, promising the medicine will shrink the white scales which will then peel off his eyes so Tobit will again see the light of day.

Anna runs out to Tobiah first and embraces him, weeping and saying now that she has seen her son, she is ready to die. Tobit stumbles through the courtyard gate to Tobiah who, with the fish gall in his hand, blows into Tobit's eyes. Holding his father firmly and telling him to have courage, he applies the medicine to his father's eyes, causing them to sting. Using both hands, he peels the white scales from the corners of Tobit's eyes. Tobit cries out weeping because he could see his son, the light of his eyes.

Tobit praises the Lord and all the Lord's holy angels. He notes God once afflicted him and God now has mercy on him. He proclaims he can now see his son, Tobiah. Tobiah tells his father about his successful journey and the return of the money and informs him he married Raguel's daughter who is soon to arrive, being near the gates of Nineveh.

At the news, Tobit goes out to greet his daughter-in-law. When the people of Nineveh see him walking so briskly with no one leading him by the hand, they are amazed. Tobit proclaims to all of them the Lord had shown mercy and opened his eyes. When Tobit meets Sarah, he blesses and welcomes her as a daughter. He blesses God, Sarah's father and mother, Tobiah, and Sarah and welcomes her into her home.

All the Jews in Nineveh rejoice. The legendary Ahiqar and his nephew Nadin, also rejoice with Tobit. In the story of Tobit, the author writes as though the betrayal of Ahiqar had not yet happened. Everyone celebrated Tobiah's wedding for seven days, and he received many gifts.

### Lectio Divina

Spend 8 to 10 minutes in silent contemplation of the following passage:

Tobit and Anna felt great anxiety when Tobiah did not arrive as expected. The passage reminds us of our human condition. Faith does not remove the anxiety many people feel when a relative or friend is sick, or someone is missing, or we experience some physical pain or distress. Mary, the mother of Jesus, said to Jesus when he was lost as a twelve-year-old for three days in Jerusalem, "Your father and I have been looking for you with great anxiety" (Luke 2:48). When people of faith experience anxiety, they resort to prayer.

✠ *What can I learn from this passage?*

## Day 3: Raphael Reveals His Identity (12)

When the wedding celebration ended, Tobit instructs Tobiah to pay the promised wages and bonus to the man who traveled with him. Tobiah asks how much he should pay, suggesting it would be well to give Raphael half the wealth he brought back with him. Since he brought Tobiah safely home and healed Sarah and Tobit, Tobiah believes this would be a bonus Raphael certainly deserves. The amount Tobiah proposes would be half of the money from Gabael and half of the wealth he received from Raguel. Tobit, who already showed himself to be a generous person, immediately agrees. Tobiah then offers Raphael half of the wealth from their trip as his wages.

Speaking to Tobiah and Tobit privately, Raphael directs them to bless and thank the Lord in song before everyone for the good things the Lord has done for them. He stresses his message by repeating it a second time, telling them to proclaim with honor all the deeds of God and not to weaken in continually offering thanks to God.

Raphael adds a short list of wisdom sayings to his message. Aware Tobit once served a king and learned many secrets of the royal court, Raphael declares a king's secret should remain a secret, but people must reveal the works of God with due honor. He tells them if they perform good works, evil will not conquer them. Prayer with fasting is good. Almsgiving with righteousness is better than wealth with wickedness and better than storing up gold. Almsgiving saves people from spiritual death and purges all sins. The almsgiver will enjoy a full life. Those who sin and perform evil deeds are their own worst enemies.

Raphael informs Tobit and Tobiah he will now reveal the whole truth to them. He repeats his wise saying about keeping a king's secret and declaring the works of God with due honor. He will now declare the works of God. He tells Tobit and Tobiah he presented their prayer and the prayer of Sarah before the Glory of God, and he likewise presented Tobit's good deed of burying the dead before God. When Tobit promptly left his dinner to bury a dead man, the Lord sent Raphael to test Tobit. The test refers to Tobit's blindness. Raphael adds the Lord also sent him to heal Tobit and Sarah. He finally reveals he is Raphael, one of the seven angels who serve before the Glory of the Lord. The names of two other angels are found in the Book of Daniel, namely Gabriel (Daniel 8:16) and Michael (Daniel 10:13). Some commentators consider the number seven in this passage to be a symbolic number representing perfection.

Tobit and Tobiah respond in the customary manner before a heavenly visitation by prostrating in fear. Raphael gives the customary response in such circumstances, telling them not to fear and offering a greeting of peace. He again bids them to bless God. The call to praise God will be repeated by Raphael as though it is a refrain in the midst of his message. Acknowledging he was not acting on his own but by God's will, Raphael again tells them to praise and thank God. Since the people of ancient times did not believe angels had to eat or drink, Raphael decides to tell them his act of eating and drinking during the trip was a vision. He announces he will soon ascend and directs them to write down all that happened to them as he ascends out of sight. Since the ancients believed God lived above the firmament, any form of disappearance would appear to be an ascension.

Tobit and Tobiah kept singing praises and offering thanks for all God did for them in the presence of the angel of the Lord.

### *Lectio Divina*

Spend 8 to 10 minutes in silent contemplation of the following passage:

> When we pray the Lord's Prayer, we name God and say, "hallowed (holy) be your name." In our prayer in honor of Mary, we pray, "Hail Mary, full of grace." Both prayers begin as prayers of praise. For Raphael, Tobit, and Tobiah, prayers of praise are esteemed as a high form of prayer. Whenever we pray, we begin by offering prayers of praise as the ancients did.

✠ *What can I learn from this passage?*

## Day 4: Tobit's Song of Praise (13)

The author pens a hymn of praise. Although the story in the Book of Tobit takes place in Nineveh during the period of an Assyrian exile of the people of the northern kingdom of Israel, the author is writing from the vantage point of a second-century Jerusalem, which means he already knows the history and difficulties the Israelites experienced from the Assyrian exile to his present day. The hymn has two divisions. The first division (verses 1–8) is a song of praise that reflects many of the themes found in the psalms and speaks of God's mercy and sings praise to the Lord. The second division (verses 9–18) is addressed to Jerusalem and recalls the prophets who foretold a new and ideal Jerusalem.

Tobit begins by singing a song of joy and praise for the Lord. He will repeat his joy and praise for the Lord throughout his prayer. He blesses the Lord, whose kingship will last forever. The Israelites considered the Lord to be the true king of Israel. From his own experiences, he can say the Lord afflicts people and shows mercy. The Lord casts people down to Hades and brings them back from the great abyss. He is not speaking of death but a dark, physical, and emotional experience such as he had with his blindness.

Tobit proclaims nothing can be snatched from the hand of God. Since he is praying in exile, he urges the Israelites to offer praise to the greatness of God in the midst of the nations because the Lord is their God and Father forever. Following a basic theme of the prophets and the psalms, Tobit notes the Lord afflicts the people when they sin, but the Lord also relents and treats them mercifully when they repent. Urging the people to consider all the Lord has done for them and to offer thanks, he bids them to bless and exalt the Lord, the King of the ages.

Tobit declares he can still thank the Lord in his captivity and proclaim the power and majesty of God to the sinful nation of his exile. Urging the people to do what is right before God who may pardon them, he exalts God, the King of heaven and rejoices in the Lord all the days of his life. He invites everyone to join him in singing praise to God in Jerusalem.

At the mention of the name "Jerusalem," the song turns its attention to the holy city. Tobit speaks of Jerusalem as though he is speaking of a person. He predicts the Lord will afflict Jerusalem, the holy city, for her sinful works but will show pity for the children of the righteous. He urges Jerusalem to offer thanks to the Lord with righteousness and praise the King of the ages so that her tabernacle (the Temple) may be rebuilt in her with joy. The author of the Book of Tobit, speaking as though he is living before the return of the Israelites from exile, already knows the Temple has been built.

Tobit prays the Lord will bring joy to all who are captives in the city and cherish for generations to come all within her who are distressed. Jerusalem will be a beacon of light for many nations, leading them from faraway lands to her holy name. The nations will bear gifts for the King of heaven, and generation after generation will offer joyful worship in her, making her name great forever and ever.

Tobit curses those who despise, scorn, hate, abuse, or destroy the city. He curses those who tear down its walls and tower and set fires to her homes. He calls for a blessing on those who respect Jerusalem. Tobit calls upon the city to rejoice over the children of the righteous who will be gathered together and will bless the Lord of the ages. He praises those who love her, rejoice in her peace, and grieve over her afflictions. They will rejoice over Jerusalem and witness her joy forever. Jerusalem will be rebuilt as the Lord's house forever. Tobit will rejoice if a remnant of his offspring survives to witness the glory of Jerusalem and offer thanks to the King of heaven.

Tobit pictures the ideal Jerusalem. Its gates will be sapphire and emerald, its walls will be made of precious stones, its towers built with gold, its battlements with purest gold, and its streets paved with rubies and stones of Ophir.

Tobit pictures the city itself rejoicing. Her gates shall sing hymns of joy and all houses will cry out, "Hallelujah." He again offers an eternal blessing to the Lord. In Jerusalem, the blessed will bless the holy name forever and ever.

### Lectio Divina

Spend 8 to 10 minutes in silent contemplation of the following passage:

The Israelites of the Old Testament believed the Lord caused everything that happened in life. If they were suffering, then God was angry and caused them to suffer, not to destroy them, but for the sake of repentance. In the New Testament era, people realize good and bad things happen in one's life, not because God directly wills it, but as a natural flow of life. Believers, however, pray for healing, knowing the Lord can and will help.

✠ *What can I learn from this passage?*

## Day 5: Epilogue (14)

Although the author of the Book of Tobit writes in this chapter as though he is predicting the future, he is writing from a period in history where these events already transpired. In apocalyptic writings, an author who has lived or is living through specific historical events writes as though he is living before the events take place, which makes him appear to be predicting the future. In this chapter, the author is using the same technique. He will speak of events taking place from the Assyrian conquest of the northern kingdom to the era after the Israelites' exile in Babylon. He is writing during the second century, when the Temple was restored and many of the people had returned from exile.

The epilogue tells us Tobit died at 112 and was buried with honor in Nineveh. A long life was a sign of God's favor. When Tobit was fifty-eight years old, he lost his sight, and after he was healed, he lived a life of prosperity. Throughout his life, he was generous in giving alms. He continued to fear the Lord and often thanked the Lord, spoken of in the text as the "divine Majesty."

On his deathbed, Tobit commands Tobiah to take his seven sons and the rest of his family and flee into Media. He claims he believes the words of

Nahum and the prophets about the destruction of Nineveh. Nahum was a minor prophet who wrote in the seventh century before Christ. All will take place as the prophets declared. Tobit tells Tobiah he will find greater safety in Media than in Assyria or Babylon. Babylon was destroyed many years after the destruction of Assyria, but the author of Tobit seems to put them in close proximity to each other.

Tobit predicts his kindred and all who dwell in Israel will be scattered and taken into exile. The land of Israel, including Samaria (the northern kingdom) and Jerusalem will then become a wilderness. He predicts the house of God (the Temple) will become desolate and be burned, but God will show mercy and bring the people back to the land of Israel. The house of God will be rebuilt, but it will not be like the first Temple until the appointed times. After the exile, all of the Israelites will return from captivity and will rebuild Jerusalem and the Temple, as the prophets foretold. All the nations will cast away their idols and reverence God in truth.

Tobit declares all nations will praise the Lord of Israel, and all the Israelites faithful to the Lord will be gathered together and come to Jerusalem and dwell in security in the land of Abraham. Those who love God sincerely will rejoice, and those who sin will disappear completely from the land.

Tobit commands Tobiah and his children to serve God sincerely and live a life faithful to the Lord, instructing their children to do what is just, give alms, remain faithful to the Lord, and bless the Lord at all times. He again reminds Tobiah to leave Nineveh, saying the day he buries his mother he should immediately leave the city. Tobiah is aware of the immense wickedness and treachery in the city, where the people sin without shame.

Tobit seeks to instill the rewards of almsgiving into Tobiah and his seven sons. Referring to the story of Ahiqar and Nadin (found in the first chapter of this book), the author of the Book of Tobit recalls how Nadin betrayed his uncle Ahiqar after Ahiqar reared him. Ahiqar had to flee and hide in a cave. Nadin's crime brought him into everlasting darkness (death), and Ahiqar came out of his cave into the light, no longer a fugitive. Tobit states it was Ahiqar's almsgiving that saved him from death. Tobit urges his children to witness the rewards of almsgiving and the punishment of the wicked.

Tobit died and was buried with honor. When Tobiah's mother died, Tobiah buried her next to his father and then departed with his wife and children for Ecbatana in Media with his father-in-law, Raguel. He cared for his father-in-law and mother-in-law until they died and buried them in Ecbatana. He inherited the estates of Raguel and Tobit. Tobiah died a highly respected man at 117. Before he died, he witnessed the destruction of Nineveh by the king of Media and praised God for all the Lord did against the Ninevites and the Assyrians.

### *Lectio Divina*

Spend 8 to 10 minutes in silent contemplation of the following passage:

The Book of Tobit ends well, continuing to stress the value of almsgiving. Jesus said, "But when you give alms, do not let your left hand know what your right is doing, so that your almsgiving may be secret. And your Father who sees in secret will repay you" (Matthew 6:3–4). God blesses those who share their gifts with others, but donors should never brag about their generosity or they will lose merit before God. Tobit was highly rewarded because he readily gave alms to those in need.

✠ *What can I learn from this passage?*

## *Review Questions*

1. What were the dangers Tobiah faced in marrying Sarah, and how were they overcome?
2. How was Tobit's blindness healed?
3. What did Raphael do for Tobiah?
4. How did Tobit know the future so well?

# The Book of Judith

## JUDITH 1–16

*I will sing a new song to my God. O Lord, great are you and glorious, marvelous in power and unsurpassable (16:13).*

**Opening Prayer** (SEE PAGE 15)

## Context

**Part 1: Judith 1—3** The Book of Judith is a legendary story about a woman named Judith, a widow much esteemed for her piety who saved the Jewish people from the Assyrian army. "Judith" means "a Jewish woman." In the story, the great general Holofernes is killed by the hand of a woman, an extraordinary disgrace in ancient times. Although written about the year 100 BC, the story reads as if it had been written when the Assyrians were a powerful nation. Because of the time span between the story and its writing, historical inaccuracies appear in the book.

In chapters 1 to 3, King Nebuchadnezzar summoned the nations west of Persia to join him in his battle against King Arphaxad of the Medes, but these nations refused to help him. After defeating King Arphaxad, Nebuchadnezzar sent his general, Holofernes, to destroy those nations who refused to fight with him.

**Part 2: Judith 4—16** Holofernes prepared to fight the Israelites at Bethulia. When Achior, the leader of the Ammonites, told Holofernes the Israelites could defeat him, he had Achior brought to the Israelites with the threat of killing him when he killed the Israelites. Judith comes as an instrument of the Lord against the army of Holofernes. Using her beauty to gain entry into the Assyrian camp, she is able to persuade Holofernes to trust her. One night, she beheads Holofernes and takes his head to her people. The death of Holofernes causes a panic among his troops, and the Israelites are able to conquer them.

## PART 1: GROUP STUDY (JUDITH 1—3)

Read aloud Judith 1—3.

### *1 Nebuchadnezzar Defeats Arphaxad*

At the beginning of the Book of Judith, the author mistakenly identifies Nebuchadnezzar as the king of the Assyrians. Nebuchadnezzar was actually the king of Babylon (604–562 BC), reigning after the destruction of Nineveh in 612 BC. The story claims to begin in the twelfth year of the reign of Nebuchadnezzar, the king of Assyria. At the time, an unknown ruler named Arphaxad ruled over the Medes in Ecbatana, a city already named in the Book of Tobit (see Tobit 5:6).

The author states Arphaxad built fortifications around Ecbatana, with walls, towers, and gates of phenomenal dimensions. The wall was 105 feet high, seventy-five feet thick, with stones four and a half feet thick and nine feet long. The tower gates measured 150 feet high and sixty feet wide.

King Nebuchadnezzar fought against King Arphaxad in the plains bordering Ragau, the home of Gabael, a relative of Tobit mentioned in the Book of Tobit. Many of the neighboring nations joined the king in his battle against Arphaxad. When Nebuchadnezzar contacted all the nations west of Persia asking for help, they refused to join him. Since the area to the west would have been named Media and not Persia before the middle of the fifth century before Christ, the author appears to be writing during the period after the Babylonian exile, unaware of the time when the Medes controlled the territory.

When the people of the land refused Nebuchadnezzar's summons, they believed they could defeat him in battle since his was only a single nation against many. They shamed the envoys sent by Nebuchadnezzar. He became enraged and swore by his throne and kingdom he would avenge their rejection.

In the seventeenth year of Nebuchadnezzar's reign, he was victorious in his battle against the forces of King Arphaxad and took possession of his cities. He invaded Ecbatana, overwhelming its towers, ransacking its marketplaces, and reducing the once-glorious city to shame. He captured Arphaxad in the mountains of Ragau and killed him. After returning triumphant to Nineveh with his large army of combined forces, he rested and feasted for 120 days.

### 2—3 Holofernes' Conquests

On the twenty-second day of the first month of Nebuchadnezzar's eighteenth year as king, he summoned all his attendants and officers and informed them about his plans to destroy the nations who refused to join him in battle. The date would coincide with the destruction of Jerusalem by the Babylonians in 587 BC.

Nebuchadnezzar summoned Holofernes, a general, who was second-in-command and told him to take 120,000 infantry and 12,000 cavalry and march against all the lands of the west because of their refusal to obey his orders. He exhorts Holofernes to tell the nations to have earth and water ready for them. During the Persian era, such an offering of land and water was a symbolic gesture, signifying the submission of the nation to a stronger army. Nebuchadnezzar promises to cover the entire land with the feet of his soldiers who will ravage them, which is another way of saying he will be sending a huge army after them. The wounded of Nebuchadnezzar's enemies will be so many they will fill the ravines and wadies. Their dead will block the swelling river, and the survivors will be sent to the ends of the earth in exile.

Nebuchadnezzar orders Holofernes to take possession of all the territories of those who refused to help him and, if they surrender, to guard them until the day of their sentencing. He is not to show mercy to those who disobeyed but kill them and plunder their land. He orders Holofernes not to disobey a single order but to fulfill the orders exactly.

Holofernes chose 120,000 skilled troops and 12,000 mounted archers and organized them for battle. After selecting many camels, donkeys, and mules to carry their supplies, he chose a multitude of sheep, cattle, and goats for food and gathered a large amount of gold and silver from the royal palace.

A large irregular force marched along with Holofernes like locusts. He traveled into the hill country and plundered cities and nations as he went through Mesopotamia, conquering every fortified city along the way to the sea. During his march, he brought fear into the heart of the inhabitants of many nations.

In chapter 3, the frightened nations sent messengers to Holofernes, humbling themselves and begging for peace. They were willing to submit themselves totally to his will, offering their dwellings, their land, their wheat, flocks, herds, and camps to Holofernes. They offered their cities and inhabitants to him to deal with as he saw fit. Holofernes received the messages and stationed his forces inside the fortified cities.

The people of the cities and the countryside received him with garlands and dancing to the sound of timbrels, but Holofernes ignored their friendly gestures and ravaged their whole territory. He destroyed their sacred groves used for the worship of false gods so the people would invoke Nebuchadnezzar as a god. The idea of invoking a ruler as a god was not a common practice until the second century before Christ, a sign the author was not familiar with the customs of the people centuries before he wrote. Holofernes eventually set up camp in the neighborhood of Dothan, a town in Ephraimite territory that once belonged in the land of the northern kingdom of Israel.

## Review Questions

1. Why is the author of Judith so confusing when speaking about Nebuchadnezzar's actual role in history?
2. Why did Nebuchadnezzar seek revenge against the people in the lands to the west?
3. What did Holofernes accomplish?

## Closing Prayer (SEE PAGE 15)

Pray the closing prayer now or after *lectio divina*.

## *Lectio Divina* (SEE PAGE 8)

Relax your body and maintain a posture of prayer (back straight, eyes shut, feet flat on the floor). This exercise can take as long as you want, but in the context of this Bible study, 10 to 20 minutes should be sufficient.

The meditations that follow are provided only to help group participants use this prayer form, but note that *lectio* is intended to bring one to a place of prayerful contemplation where the Word of God speaks to the hearer from his or her heart. (See page 8 for further instruction.)

### Nebuchadnezzar Defeats Arphaxad (1)

We all seek peace, but violence and terrorism such as that shown by Nebuchadnezzar are present in every era of history. Jesus tells us, "Peace I leave with you; my peace I give to you. Not as the world gives do I give it to you. Do not let your hearts be troubled or afraid" (John 14:27). The peace Jesus brings is a spiritual peace that can exist even where there is violence. It consists of a belief God is with us, no matter how difficult or frightening our life may be.

✠ *What can I learn from this passage?*

### Holofernes' Conquests (2—3)

Evil people like Nebuchadnezzar can always find allies, as he did with Holofernes. In the Book of Sirach, we read, "Every living thing loves its own kind, and we all love someone like ourselves" (Sirach 13:15). Evil attracts evil, and good attracts good. Following the words of Sirach, we may learn something about ourselves by the company we keep.

✠ *What can I learn from this passage?*

## PART 2: INDIVIDUAL STUDY (JUDITH 4—16)

### Day 1: Holofernes and Judea (4—5)

When the Israelites heard of the treachery of Holofernes over the nations he conquered, they became deeply frightened. They feared for themselves, for Jerusalem, and for the Temple of the Lord. The author writes that the people of Judea recently returned from exile and had purified the vessels, the altar, and the Temple. It is not clear which exile is meant. The Israelites sent word to their surrounding neighbors to fortify the hilltops and the villages on them. Only a few of the villages mentioned in the Bible passage are known.

The high priest, Joakim, who was in Jerusalem, wrote to the inhabitants, instructing them to defend the mountain passes that provided access to Judea. Since the approach was only wide enough for two at a time, they would be easy to defend.

All the people cried out fervently to the Lord and clothed themselves in sackcloth, the garment of grief and repentance. They draped sackcloth over the altar and cried out in unison to the Lord of Israel to protect them, their city, and the sanctuary. As the people of Judea continue to fast for many days before the sanctuary of the Lord in Jerusalem, the Lord hears their cry and witnesses their distress. The high priest, the priests, and those who ministered to the Lord offered the daily burnt offering, the votive offerings, and the voluntary offerings of the people. With ashes on their turbans, the usual sign of grieving and repentance, they cried out to the Lord to look with favor on Israel.

In chapter 5, Holofernes receives word the Israelites were prepared for battle. They had blocked the mountain passes, fortified the hilltops, and set up roadblocks in the plains. In a rage, Holofernes called together all the rulers of Moab, the governors of Ammon, and the satraps of the coastlands, and asked them a series of questions: "What sort of people is this that lives in the hill country? Which cities do they inhabit? How large is their force? In what does their power and strength consist? Who has set himself up as their king and the leader of their army? Why have they alone of all the inhabitants of the west refused to come out to meet me" (5:3–4)?

Achior, the leader of the Ammonites, said he will share the truth about these people. Referring to Abraham, who came from Ur of the Chaldeans, he states the people are descendants of the Chaldeans, who formerly lived in Mesopotamia and did not wish to worship the gods of their ancestors. Since they worshiped the God of heaven, their ancestors expelled them from the presence of their gods. They fled to Mesopotamia and lived there for a long time until their God told them to leave the place they were living and to go to the land of Canaan.

Achior said the people settled in Canaan and became rich in gold, silver, and an abundance of livestock. After a period of time, during a famine, they migrated to Egypt, where they remained as long as they found provisions. They multiplied to the point no one could count their number. The king of Egypt forced them into slavery. They cried out to their God, who struck the whole land of Egypt with unrelenting plagues.

When the Egyptians drove the Israelites out, their God dried up the Red Sea and led them along their route to Sinai and to Kadesh-barnea. They drove out all the people of the wilderness and settled in the land of the Amorites. Because of their might, they destroyed the Heshbonites, crossed the Jordan, and took possession of the hill country. They drove out the inhabitants of the land and lived there a long time.

Achior informed Holofernes that as long as the Israelites remained faithful to their Lord and did not sin, they would prosper. Their God, who hates wickedness, was with them. When they abandoned the commands of the Lord, they were destroyed by frequent wars and were finally taken as captives to foreign lands. The Temple of their God was totally destroyed.

Achior continued to speak, saying they returned to their God and reclaimed Jerusalem where their sanctuary (Temple) is. Because their hill country was unoccupied, they were able to settle there again. Achior tells Holofernes about the secret strength of the Israelites. If they are sinning against their God, and if this can be verified, Holofernes will be able to conquer them. If they are not guilty, then Holofernes should keep away, for the Lord, their God, will protect them, and the attackers will be mocked in the eyes of the nations.

When Achior had finished speaking, the people murmured and the officers and inhabitants of the seacoast and Moab said Achior should be cut to pieces. They declared they did not fear the Israelites whom they considered to be a weak people, incapable of a strong defense. They urged Holofernes to attack the people of Judea.

### Lectio Divina

Spend 8 to 10 minutes in silent contemplation of the following passage:

> Despite all the Jewish people have endured throughout history, their faith in the protection of God keeps Judaism thriving. Throughout the ages, like the Jewish people, Christians have struggled and died, but somehow the community of Christ is still here, more than 2,000 years later. The only explanation is the protection of the Lord.

✠ *What can I learn from this passage?*

## Day 2: Siege of Bethulia (6—7)

Holofernes asks who Achior and his followers from Ephraim are to advise him not to fight against the Israelites because the Israelite's God protects them. He asks who God is beside Nebuchadnezzar. Declaring the God of the Israelites will not save them, Holofernes boasts the servants of Nebuchadnezzar, his army, will make their mountains drunk with blood and fill the plains with their corpses so not even a trace of them will be found.

Although Achior spoke the truth, Holofernes says he (Achior) will not see him again until he has avenged himself against the people who came out of Egypt. He commands his men to escort Achior to the hill country and leave him in one of the cities near the passes. When Holofernes returns from the battle, his army will kill Achior and he will fall among the wounded Israelites. If he believes the Israelites will not fall, then he has no reason to be discouraged. His servants led Achior to the springs below Bethulia. When the Israelites saw them, they rushed out of the city to the top of the hill and all the slingers kept them from coming up by casting stones at them. Taking cover below the hill, they bound Achior and abandoned him at the bottom of the hill.

When the Israelites came down the hill, they found Achior, untied him, brought him into Bethulia, and placed him before their rulers. They hastily convened the inhabitants of the city, the elders, the young men, and the women. Uzziah, one of the rulers, questioned Achior about what happened. Achior told them all he said to Holofernes and the Assyrian rulers and the threats Holofernes breathed against Israel.

When the people heard what Achior had to say, they fell prostrate and worshiped God, begging the Lord to have mercy on them. Uzziah brought Achior to his home, where he held a banquet for the elders.

In chapter 7, Holofernes ordered all his troops and their allies to break camp and move against Bethulia. They were to seize the passes into the hills and make war on the Israelites. In the march were 170,000 infantry and 12,000 cavalry, not including the men who accompanied the baggage train on foot. Their number was so vast they covered a large mass of land, casting fear upon the Israelites who saw them. Although the Israelites became greatly distressed, they grabbed their weapons, set fires in the towers, and kept watch throughout the night.

On the second day, Holofernes reconnoitered the ascent to the city and located the springs of water used by the people. He seized them, stationed armed detachments around them, and returned to his troops. The leaders of the Edomites and the Moabites tell him not to approach the Israelites in formation to avoid losing many of their troops trying to reach the Israelites who will be fighting from the top of the mountains. They tell him the Israelites do not depend on their spears but on the height of the mountains.

The leaders of the Edomites and Moabites suggest Holofernes keep control of the springs of water and the inhabitants of Bethulia will wilt with thirst and surrender the city. In the meanwhile the leaders said they and their troops will encamp on nearby hilltops to guard against anyone leaving the city. Everyone in the city will languish with hunger and die in the streets where they live.

Holofernes and his attendants liked the proposal and decided to execute it. The Ammonites, with 5,000 Assyrians, encamped in the valley and guarded the water supply and springs of the Israelites. The Assyrian army covered the entire plain with their encampment. Their tents and equipment covered the land.

Distressed at their thirst and the surrounding enemy, the Israelites pleaded with the Lord, their God, for help. The Assyrian force kept them surrounded for thirty-four days. Their children were lethargic, and the women and youth were fainting from thirst in the streets and gateways of the city. All the people came to Uzziah and the rulers of the city claiming God had sold them into the hands of the Assyrians by laying them prostrate with thirst and exhaustion. They beg the leaders of the city to summon the Assyrians and offer them the whole city as plunder. Although they realize they would be made slaves to the Assyrians, they would at least live and not have to see their children and wives dying before their eyes.

Uzziah urged them to allow the Lord five days more to show mercy toward them. He declares the Lord will not forsake them and promises, if nothing happens in five days, he will do as they ask. The men returned to their posts on the walls and towers, and the women and children went back to their homes.

### Lectio Divina

Spend 8 to 10 minutes in silent contemplation of the following passage:

The plight of the Israelites seems so helpless, but the leaders of the people encourage them to trust God. On November 18, 2013, Pope Francis issued an exhortation titled "The Joy of the Gospel." He spoke of the need for faith and joy in the midst of suffering. He writes, "I understand the grief of people who have to endure great suffering, yet slowly but surely we all have to let the joy of faith slowly revive as a quiet yet firm trust, even amid the greatest distress." For the pope, nothing can separate us from our love for God and God's love for us.

✠ *What can I learn from this passage?*

## Day 3: Judith, Instrument of the Lord (8—10:10)

Judith is sent by the Lord. Her husband died in Bethulia, his native city, at the time of a barley harvest when he was overcome by the heat supervising those binding sheaves. Judith lived at home as a widow for three years and four months. In mourning, she set up a tent on her roof, put sackcloth around her waist, and wore widow's clothing. She fasted every day except on the eve of the Sabbath and the Sabbath itself, the eve of new moons and new moons, and on the days of religious festivals. She was a very beautiful woman. Her husband left her gold and silver, male and female servants, livestock and fields, which she maintained. No one said anything bad about her, for she feared God greatly.

Judith berated Uzziah and the leaders for swearing to the people they would turn over the city to the Assyrians in five days if God did not respond to their prayers. She accused them of putting God to the test. Since they are unable to plumb the depths of the human heart or know the workings of the human mind, how can they understand God, who made all these things, or understand God's plan? They should not impose conditions on the plans of God. Judith declares the worship of gods made by hand does not exist in the manner it did in former days. Because of their worship of false gods, their ancestors were killed and plundered. In light of the reality they no longer worship false gods, Judith's hope is the Lord will not reject the people of Israel.

Judith knows if Bethulia allows itself to be captured, all of Judea will fall, the sanctuary will be plundered, and God will hold them accountable among the nations for the slaughter of their kindred and for the wreckage of their heritage. The people will be a shame in the eyes of those who enslave them.

Judith calls upon the rulers to join her in being an example for their kindred whose life, sanctuary, Temple, and altar depend on them. Choosing to view their current difficulty in a different manner, she bids them to offer thanks to the Lord for putting them to the test as God did with their ancestors. She urges them to recall how the Lord dealt with Abraham, Isaac, and Jacob while he was tending the flocks of Laban, his mother's brother.

Uzziah agrees with Judith and praises her for her wisdom, noting this was not the first time her wisdom became evident. All the people recognized her wisdom from her earliest days and witnessed the goodness of her heart. Uzziah claims the thirst of the people forced him and the leaders to bind themselves by an oath they cannot break. Noting Judith's godliness, he begs her to pray for them so the Lord will send rain to fill up their cisterns.

Judith predicts she will perform a deed that will go down from generation to generation. She directs them to stand at the city gates and allow her to pass through with her maid, promising the Lord will deliver Israel within the number of the days they specified for their surrender. She says they should not inquire what she will be doing because she will not tell them until it is accomplished.

In chapter 9, Judith prepared for prayer by falling prostrate, putting ashes on her head, and uncovering the sackcloth she was wearing. Judith cried out to the Lord at the time of evening worship in the Temple when incense was being offered to God in Jerusalem.

Judith prayed to the Lord, the God of her father, Simeon, into whose hand God put a sword to avenge the foreigners who defiled a virgin by violating her, shaming her by uncovering her thighs, and dishonoring her by polluting (opening) her womb. When she speaks of Simeon as her father, she means he is one of her ancestors. This is a reference to the story in Genesis. Shechem, a Hivite, raped Dinah, a daughter of Jacob, and later wanted to marry her. Jacob's sons said they could not allow Shechem to marry her unless he and all the males among the Hivites were circumcised. The Hivites agreed and were circumcised. On the third day, while they were still in pain and helpless, Simeon and Levi killed them all with their swords. All the brothers plundered the land (see Genesis 34).

She speaks of the Assyrians' pride in their horses, chariots, troops, and weapons, unaware the Lord does not need an army. Because the Assyrians planned to profane the sanctuary, defile the Temple, and destroy the altar, Judith prays the Lord will shatter their strength and crush their army. She prays she will have a strong hand to execute her plan. When she prays the Lord will crush the arrogance of the Assyrians, she prays it will be done by her hand, the hand of a female. In a male-oriented society, death of a warrior at the hand of a woman is a huge disgrace.

God is a God of the lowly, a helper of those who account for little, a support for the weak, a protector of those in despair, and a savior of those without hope. She pleads with the Lord, saying the Lord is the heritage of Israel, the Master of heaven and earth, the Creator of the waters, and the King of all the Lord created. She prays her deceitful words will wound and bruise those who have planned wickedness against the Lord's covenant, the holy Temple, Mount Zion, and all of Judah. At the end of the prayer, she prays her deeds will bring glory to God. She prays every nation and every tribe will know clearly the God of Israel is truly God, a God of power and might, and a God like no other who shields the people of Israel.

In chapter 10, when Judith finished praying, she called her maid and went into the house she used only on Sabbaths and feast days. She removed her sackcloth and the garments of widowhood. She washed herself, anointed herself with rich oil, arranged her hair, put on a diadem, and dressed in the festive clothing she wore when her husband was alive. She put on sandals, anklets, bracelets, rings, earrings, and all her other jewelry. She made herself enticing for the eyes of all the men who see her. Giving her maid a skin of wine and a jug of oil, she filled a bag with roasted grain, dried fig cakes, and pure bread. She then wrapped all her dishes and gave them to her maid to carry.

Judith and her maid went to the gate of the city and found Uzziah and the elders of the city standing there. When they saw Judith, they were astounded at her beauty. They prayed the God of their ancestors would grant her favor and make her plan successful for the glory of the Israelites and Jerusalem.

She gave orders for the gate to be opened. They ordered the young men to open the gate for her, and Judith and her maid went out. The men kept her in view as she went down the mountain and crossed the valley, where they lost sight of her.

### Lectio Divina

Spend 8 to 10 minutes in silent contemplation of the following passage:

Judith is an example of one who trusts God to the point of being ready to die for the Lord if she must. She was concerned both about saving her life and protecting the Temple and the name of the Lord. Throughout history, brave men and women have faced death for the sake of helping the poor, worshiping God, or preaching Jesus' message. A difficult question for all of us is whether we would be willing to offer our life as these brave martyrs have done.

✠ *What can I learn from this passage?*

## Day 4: Judith Goes Out to War (10:11—13)

As Judith and her maid walked across the valley, an Assyrian patrol stopped them and asked her who her people were, where she came from, and where she was going. She told them she was a daughter of the Hebrews, fleeing from them because they were about to be plundered by them. She said she came to see Holofernes and give him a trustworthy report, showing him the way he can ascend and take possession of the whole city without any in their army being wounded or killed. .

When the men on patrol heard her words and beheld her marvelously beautiful face, they said she saved her life by leaving the Israelite camp to come and see their master. They accompanied her with 100 men to the tent of Holofernes. They told her not to fear when she comes before him and tells him what she had told them.

As the news of her arrival spread among the tents, a crowd gathered around her as she waited outside Holofernes' tent. When the crowd saw her beauty, they had a different opinion about the Israelites, asking who could despise a nation with such a beautiful woman among them. In their mind, if the others were as beautiful as she, they would kill the men and spare the women for themselves.

Holofernes' guards and all his attendants came out of the tent and ushered her into it. Holofernes was reclining on his bed under a canopy woven of purple, gold, emeralds, and other precious stones. When they announced her arrival, he came out to the front part of the tent, preceded by silver lamps. Holofernes and his attendants marveled at the beauty of Judith's face. When she fell prostrate and paid him homage, Holofernes' servants raised her up.

In chapter 11, Holofernes tells Judith to have no fear, saying he never hurt anyone who chose to serve Nebuchadnezzar, king of the earth. Since the author relates in 3:2–8 about Holofernes destroying a nation of people who claimed to be servants of Nebuchadnezzar, this statement is obviously false. Holofernes tells Judith he would not have raised a sword against her people if they had not insulted him. Assuring her she came in safety, he asked her to tell him why she fled from her people and came to them.

Judith promises to say nothing false to "my lord." The author appears to be giving the word "lord" a double meaning, referring to Holofernes and God. Her words are true if understood properly. If Holofernes follows her directions, God will successfully perform a deed through him and the designs of the "lord" will not fail. What Holofernes interprets as plans for his success is really a reference to the plans of the Lord God that will be successful in saving the Israelites. Judith swears by the life of Nebuchadnezzar, king of all the earth, and by the power of the one whom all humans and animals serve and who guides all living things. The one who guides all living things is a veiled reference to God, who is served not only by human beings but also by all animals on earth and in the air. Holofernes is unable to understand the double meaning in Judith's words and believes she is speaking about Nebuchadnezzar.

Judith praises Holofernes as wise and clever, with a reputation before all the earth of being capable, experienced, and distinguished in military strategy. Her praise about the exceptional abilities of Holofernes will demonstrate more forcefully the great power of the God of the Israelites when Holofernes is defeated.

Judith tells Holofernes the Israelites learned about the message Achior gave to Holofernes' council. She expresses her agreement with Achior's words about the Lord protecting the Israelites when they do not sin and punishing them when they do sin. According to Judith, the Israelites are now planning to sin by alleviating their hunger with animals the Law forbids them to eat. They will also eat the grain, and drink wine and oil which were consecrated and set aside for the priests who minister before God in Jerusalem. Since the people in Jerusalem were already doing this, the people of Bethulia sent messengers to receive permission from the religious leaders in Jerusalem. She says once the people respond to this permission, they will act upon it and sin. The Lord will then turn them over to Holofernes for destruction.

Judith feigns fear of being killed, saying when she learned of the sin of the people she knew God would no longer protect them, so she fled. She declares God sent her to Holofernes to perform deeds that will astonish the nations who hear about it. Holofernes interprets her words to mean she will help him conquer the Israelites, when she is actually saying his death will be the cause of the astonishment of the nations. Judith claims she is a God-fearing woman who wishes to go out into the valley each night to pray, saying God will tell her in prayer when the Israelites have committed their sin. In going out to pray each night, Judith is establishing a means of escape when Holofernes is killed.

When the Israelites commit their sin, Judith will tell Holofernes so he can march out with his forces. She promises to lead him through to the heart of

Judea until he arrives in Jerusalem, where she will set up his throne. Her words are true, but not in the sense believed by Holofernes. When she returns to Judea, she will "lead" his head through Judea to Jerusalem where his head will be enthroned for all to see.

Holofernes and all his attendants marveled at Judith's wisdom, not knowing her wisdom will make fools of them. Holofernes declares Judith is not only beautiful but wise. He promises that if all turns out as she predicts, her God will be his God. In reality, his death will show the power of her God over him. He tells her she will live in the palace of King Nebuchadnezzar and be renowned throughout the earth. Since her actions will be known in the palace of King Nebuchadnezzar and nations throughout the earth will recall the exploits of the woman who killed Holofernes, her name will indeed be renowned.

In chapter 12, Holofernes ordered his attendants to lead Judith into the room with his silver dinnerware and provide her with his food and wine for her table. Refusing to eat or drink because it would be a sin for her, she tells Holofernes she brought enough supplies with her. When Holofernes asks what will happen when her supplies run out, she tells him they will not run out before the Lord accomplishes by her hand what is to be done.

In the morning, she sent a message to Holofernes asking him to give orders allowing her to go out for prayer. For three days, she went out at night to the valley of Bethulia, where she bathed. The bathing was a necessary ritual because of her contact with Gentiles. She returned to her tent and remained there until her food was brought to her toward evening.

On the fourth day, Holofernes gave a banquet for his servants. He ordered Bagoas, the eunuch in charge of his personal affairs, to persuade Judith to eat and drink with him, saying it would be a shame to be with such a beautiful woman and not enjoy her company. Bagoas invited her to come and act like one of the Assyrian woman in the palace of Nebuchadnezzar. Judith accepted the invitation with great enthusiasm, declaring this will be a joy for her until the day of her death.

Judith was dressed in her festive garments and all her finery. During the meal, Holofernes burned with passion. When Holofernes urged her to drink and be happy with them, she responded this day was the greatest day of her life. She was referring to the death of Holofernes. Her maid supplied her with her food and drink. Holofernes drank heavily, more than at any other time.

In chapter 13, after all the attendants left, Judith remained with Holofernes, who was sprawled out on the bed, drunk from too much wine. Judith ordered her maidservant to stand outside and told Bagoas she would be going out for her usual prayer later. Alone in the tent with Holofernes, Judith prayed for the Lord, God of all might, to look graciously on the deed she was about to perform for the exaltation of Jerusalem. She took Holofernes' sword from the bedpost near the head of Holofernes, grabbed him by the hair, prayed for strength, and struck Holofernes' neck twice with all her might, cutting off his head. She rolled the body off the bed and took the canopy from its posts. Shortly after, she came out and handed Holofernes' head to her maid, who put it into her food bag. The two went out to pray as they ordinarily did.

Judith and her maid passed through the camp, skirted the valley, and went up the mountain to Bethulia. Approaching the gates, she shouted for the guards to open the gates, saying God, their God, was with them and has once more shown his power in Israel against the enemy. All the people hurriedly assembled, astounded at her return. She took the head out of her bag, showed it to the people and announced it was Holofernes' head. The most humiliating and shameful form of death was death at the hands of a woman. Judith announces the Lord struck Holofernes down by the hand of a female. She explained Holofernes did not defile her, but it was the beauty of her face that seduced him.

The people praised God for humiliating the enemy of the Israelites. Uzziah declared her deed would never be forgotten by those aware of the power of God. Because she risked her life when the people were being oppressed, he prays her deed will redound to her everlasting honor and the Lord will reward her with blessings. All the people answered, "Amen! Amen!"

## *Lectio Divina*

Spend 8 to 10 minutes in silent contemplation of the following passage:

An enemy soldier, who divulged classified information to his mistress who was a spy, was arrested and sentenced to death. Before he died, a newspaper reporter asked him why he divulged the information to the woman. He responded, "I just lost my head over her." Whenever people commit any form of sin, we can say they "lost their head" and turned against God. Holofernes literally lost his head over Judith. Uzziah, in response to her deed, praised her when he spoke words we would all hope to live by when he said she walked "in the straight path before our God" (13:20).

✠ *What can I learn from this passage?*

## Day 5: Victory and Thanksgiving (14—16)

Judith ordered the people to take the head of Holofernes and hang it on the wall of the city. At daybreak, they are to take their weapons and rush out of the city under the command of a captain as though they are about to go down into the valley against the Assyrians. They are not to go down. The Assyrians will seize their weapons and hurry to their camp to awaken their generals. Panic will seize them when they rush to the tent of Holofernes and do not find him. At that point, the Israelites and their allies are to pursue them and strike them dead.

Judith asked for Achior to be led to her. When Achior saw the head of Holofernes in the hand of one of the men in the assembly, he fainted. The people most likely never saw Holofernes' face, but Achior did. His fainting verifies for the people Judith really returned with the head of Holofernes.

When Achior recovered, he asked Judith to tell him all she did during those days in the camp of Holofernes, and Judith told him in the presence of all the people. Seeing all the Lord had done through Judith, Achior believed in the God of Israel and circumcised his flesh and united himself with the house of Israel.

At dawn, they hung the head of Holofernes on the wall and the Israelites charged to the mountain passes. The Assyrians notified their commanders, who in turn notified their generals and other leaders the Israelites, referred to as slaves by the army, were coming to battle them. When they came to Holofernes' tent and called out to him, they received no answer. Bagoas parted the curtain gingerly, thinking Holofernes was in bed with Judith. Instead, he found Holofernes' body on the floor without his head. He let out a loud cry and tore his garments as a sign of scandal and sadness. He rushed to the tent of Judith and found it empty. Going out, he reported the slaves have tricked them. A single Hebrew woman brought shame on the house of King Nebuchadnezzar. The leaders of the Assyrian forces became distressed, tore their tunics, and wailed throughout the camp.

In chapter 15, those in the encampments broke ranks and fled in all directions, and those stationed in the hills around Bethulia also fled. The Israelite warriors pursued them. Uzziah sent messengers to the whole territory of Israel to call them to join in destroying the enemy. The remaining people of Bethulia and all the returning Israelites plundered the camp of the Assyrians, acquiring a huge amount of wealth.

The high priest Joakim and the senate of the Israelites who lived in Jerusalem came and praised Judith, calling her the glory of Jerusalem, the great pride of Israel, and the great boast of their nation. They pray the Almighty Lord will bless her forever. All the people responded, "Amen."

For thirty days all the people plundered the camp and gave Holofernes' tent, dishes, and furniture to Judith. She distributed branches to the women who gathered to bless and dance with her. They were followed by the men bearing their weapons, wearing garlands, and singing songs of praise.

In chapter 16, Judith sang a song of praise to God and the Israelites, with tambourines and cymbals, joined in praising the Lord. They sang the Lord is a God who crushes wars and encamps among the people, the one who delivered Judith from her pursuers. The huge number of Assyrians covered the wadis and hills, threatening to burn their territory, kill their youth, seize the children, and carry off their virgins. The Lord, however, defeated them by the hand of a female.

Although the song is attributed to Judith, the author speaks in the prayer about Judith who brought the enemy down by her beauty, removing her widow's garb and dressing in attractive finery. The Persians and Medes admired her daring.

The poem shifts back to Judith as the speaker. She sings of the weak ones crying out and spearing the terrified enemy who perished before the Lord. Judith sings a new song, praising the Lord for the Lord's marvelous gifts. She proclaims the mercy that is given to those who fear the Lord. Fear of the Lord is greater than offering sacrifices to the Lord. Judith sends a warning to the people who would rise against her people, saying they will be punished by the Almighty who will send fire and worms in their flesh.

When the people arrived in Jerusalem, they worshiped God. Judith then dedicated to God Holofernes' canopy, putting it under the ban. Judith and the people celebrated for three months in Jerusalem.

Judith went back to live in Bethulia. She refused those who wished to marry her and her fame continued to spread. She freed her maidservant and died at 105, a sign of God's favor. She was buried with her husband, Manasseh.

### Lectio Divina

Spend 8 to 10 minutes in silent contemplation of the following passage:

> Judith performed an amazing triumph for the Israelites and became widely known and praised. Her faith, however, kept her humble. Whenever she received praise, she always turned her praise into praise for the Lord. She teaches us how foolish it is to become proud of our gifts as though we are responsible for them. We build on the gifts the Lord gives us—with the help of the Lord.

✠ *What can I learn from this passage?*

## Review Questions

1. Who was Achior and what did he do?
2. What was Holofernes' plan in conquering the Israelites?
3. How did Judith disgrace Holofernes?
4. In what ways did Judith show her wisdom?

# The Book of Esther

## ESTHER (A) 1–10 (F)

*These days of Purim were never to be neglected among the Jews, nor forgotten by their descendants (9:28).*

**Opening Prayer** (SEE PAGE 15)

## Context

**Part 1: Esther (A) 1—2** The story in the Book of Esther takes place under a Persian emperor known as King Ahasuerus, whose rule is loosely based on the rule of King Xerxes (485 to 464 BC). The book was originally written in Hebrew and later translated into Greek with some additions. It was written in the third or second century before Christ, long before the events it portrays. The Greek additions are indicated in the *New American Bible,* revised edition, by the letters "A" to "F." The original Hebrew makes no mention of God, but the Greek additions mention God or Lord more than fifty times. On a few occasions, the Greek author adds the name of God in the midst of the Hebrew text.

The opening chapters of the book introduce the reader to a man named Mordecai who has a confusing dream that will not be interpreted until the end of the book. He is favored by the king when he reveals an assassination plot against him (the king). When the queen refuses a command by the king, he rejects her and chooses Esther as his queen.

**Part 2: Esther 3—10 (F)** The story in these chapters begins before Mordecai finds favor with the king. Haman, second-in-charge after the king, seeks to destroy Mordecai and all the Jews. With the help of Esther, Mordecai is able to overcome Haman and save the Jews from annihilation. The Jews celebrate the event of his salvation every year as the feast of Purim.

## PART 1: GROUP STUDY (ESTHER [A] 1—2)

Read aloud Esther (A) 1—2.

### (A) Prologue: Dream of Mordecai

Chapter A is a Greek addition to the Hebrew Book of Esther. The book opens in the second year of Ahasuerus the Great, on the first day of Nisan. The date refers to the year 485, in the month of March. On that day, a central character of the book named Mordecai, has a dream. The name "Mordecai" comes from the name of the Babylonian god Marduk. The genealogy of Mordecai connects him with the tribe of Saul, who was the son of a man named Kish (see 1 Samuel 9:1–2) and who belonged to the tribe of Benjamin. According to the genealogy of Mordecai, Kish would be the great-grandfather of Mordecai.

Mordecai was a Jew residing in the city of Susa who served in the king's court and was one of the captives Nebuchadnezzar of Babylon marched from Jerusalem with King Jeconiah, king of Judah. This took place in 587 BC. In 2 Kings, Jeconiah is referred to as Jehoiachin, who was deported by the king of Babylon with his family and court (see 2 Kings 24:15). If the date given in the first verse were true (485 BC) and the date of the Babylonian captivity was 587 BC, then Mordecai would be more than 100 years old, which is unlikely. The author is apparently not concerned about the inconsistency when he speaks of the era of Mordecai.

Mordecai had a disturbing dream that is described in apocalyptic terms. In his dream, there is loud thunder and an earthquake. On a dark and dismal day, two huge dragons appeared poised for battle. Dragons are found in apocalyptic writings, although the dragons in this story are not both evil as they usually are in apocalyptic writings. One is evil and the other is good. They thundered with a deafening cry which drove the nations of the wicked to prepare for a battle against the nation of the just. Anguish and distress, evil and great confusion covered the earth. Believing they would perish, the nation of the just shook with fear at the evil in store for them. The people cried out to God. From their screaming, a mighty river, a flood of water, arose as though from a tiny spring. The light of the sun broke through and the lowly were exalted. They devoured those who boasted. Having seen in this dream what the Lord intended, Mordecai awoke and tried throughout the day to interpret it. He will be able to interpret the dream at the end of the Book of Esther.

Mordecai rested in a courtyard with two eunuchs of the king who guarded the courtyard. One day, when he heard them plotting, he investigated and discovered they were planning to kill King Ahasuerus. He informed the king, who ordered them to be questioned. When they confessed their plot, the king condemned them to death. Both the king and Mordecai recorded these things in writing. As a reward for Mordecai's actions, the king appointed him to serve in his court.

A rogue named Haman, a Bougean, and a man held in high honor by the king, sought to harm Mordecai and his people due to the failure of the eunuch's plot to kill the king. The tribe, Bougean, appears to refer to an "Agagite," a term which associates him with the Amalekite king, Agag, defeated by Saul, a fellow tribesman of Mordecai. The author pictures the tribe of Saul still in conflict with the Amalekites, represented by Haman.

### 1—2 Choosing a New Queen

The Persian King Ahasuerus—whom the author states ruled over 127 provinces while in reality he ruled over only about thirty—gave a feast for all his official ministers and friends. This feast lasted for 180 days, and the guests included army officers, nobles, and governors from Persia and Media. The guests at such feasts ordinarily would stay for a designated period of time and others would be invited to take their place in an orderly fashion. During the feast, King Ahasuerus exhibited the magnificent riches of his kingdom and the dazzling riches of his imperial estate. The author describes the elaborate cotton draperies and hangings, gold and silver couches on a mosaic pavement of expensive stones. The wine was abundant, as was the custom at such feasts. The queen hosted a feast for the women in the royal palace.

On the seventh day, when the king was drunk with wine, he sent seven of his eunuchs to bring Queen Vashti into his presence wearing the royal crown. He wanted to display her beauty to the people and officials. When the queen refused the royal order, the king burned with fury. He conferred with the sages and the seven Persian and Mede officials who personally served the king and asked what was to be done with the queen for disobeying the order.

The queen's refusal was viewed as a possible rebellion of all the women. A man named Memucan, speaking on behalf of the seven, said if the king did nothing and the women learned of it, they would disregard their own husbands. They advised the king to send out a royal decree, forbidding the queen from coming into his presence and authorizing the king to give her royal dignity to one more worthy. This will lead wives to honor their husbands. The idea pleased the king and he sent letters to all the people in their own language, saying the man should be lord in his own home.

In chapter 2, the king's personal attendants suggested beautiful young virgins be gathered into the harem for the king by the king's emissaries. They suggested the king direct the eunuch to give cosmetics to the women, and the woman who pleases the king shall reign in place of Vashti. This suggestion pleased the king.

In Susa was a Jew named Mordecai of the line of Kish of the tribe of Benjamin taken captive with Jeconiah, the king of Judah, whom Nebuchadnezzar exiled to Babylon. The reader will notice this genealogy of Mordecai is similar to that found in A, verse 1. Since the Greek-lettered chapters in the Book of Esther were written after the Hebrew edition of the letter, commentators recognize the similar Greek passages were taken from the Hebrew passages.

Mordecai, who was Esther's cousin, became her foster father when she lost her parents. She was lovely and beautiful. At the death of her mother and father, Mordecai adopted her as his own daughter. When the royal decree brought all the women of the kingdom together, Esther was brought to the royal palace under the care of Hegai, guardian of the women. When Esther won his favor, he promptly furnished her with cosmetics and provisions. He chose seven maids for her and placed them in the best place in the harem.

Mordecai commanded her not to reveal her nationality or family. Each day, he would walk around in front of the harem to learn how Esther was doing and what was to happen to her.

After the twelve months of preparation decreed for the women, each one in turn visited the king. The woman could take with her from the harem whatever she wished. She went in the evening and returned in the morning to a second harem under the care of the royal eunuch, the guardian of the concubines. She could not return to the king unless he was pleased and summoned her by name. When Esther's turn came, she did not ask for anything but what Hegai, the guardian of the women, suggested. She won the admiration of all who saw her.

After Esther was led to the king, he loved her more than all the other women, and of all the virgins she won his favor and goodwill. He placed the crown on her head and made her queen in place of Vashti. The king honored Esther with a grand feast, granted a holiday to the provinces, and gave generous gifts.

Esther still did not reveal her family or nationality because Mordecai told her not to. She followed Mordecai's instructions as she did when he raised her. During the time Mordecai spent at the king's gate, he overheard two eunuchs guarding the entrance who were angry with the king, plotting to assassinate him. Mordecai told Queen Esther of the plot, who in turn informed the king in Mordecai's name. When the matter was investigated and verified, both eunuchs were impaled on stakes. This event was copied and repeated in a different manner in A:12—17. In the king's presence, this was inscribed in the annals.

## *Review Questions*

1. What is the first story about the king rewarding Mordecai?
2. How did Esther become a queen?
3. What is the second story about the king rewarding Mordecai?

**Closing Prayer** (SEE PAGE 15)

Pray the closing prayer now or after *lectio divina*.

## *Lectio Divina* (SEE PAGE 8)

Relax your body and maintain a posture of prayer (back straight, eyes shut, feet flat on the floor). This exercise can take as long as you want, but in the context of this Bible study, 10 to 20 minutes should be sufficient.

The meditations that follow are provided only to help group participants use this prayer form, but note that *lectio* is intended to bring one to a place of prayerful contemplation where the Word of God speaks to the hearer from his or her heart. (See page 8 for further instruction.)

### Prologue: Dream of Mordecai (A)

In Mordecai's dream, the image of two dragons, one good and the other evil, illustrates the ongoing struggle in creation between good and evil. Christians believe good triumphs over evil in the end. Jesus confronted evil and showed us the value of remaining faithful in the Lord, no matter how difficult.

✠ *What can I learn from this passage?*

### Choosing a New Queen (1—2)

It is difficult to decide how much God has to do with our life-changing events. God uses the choice of Esther as queen to save the Jews, but she had no idea what God had in mind for her. God guides us, but it is still up to us to respond to God's promptings. People pray for discernment to be able to respond to God's will.

✠ *What can I learn from this passage?*

# PART 2: INDIVIDUAL STUDY (ESTHER 3—10 [F])

### Day 1: Mordecai and Haman (3—B)

King Ahasuerus promoted Haman to a high rank above all his fellow officials. The king ordered all the king's servants at the royal gate to kneel and bow to Haman. Mordecai, however, refused to kneel and bow down to him. The others at the gate kept asking Mordecai why he disobeyed the king's order, and he answered he was a Jew. Later in the book, Mordecai will reveal he only bows down to the Lord. They informed Haman about Mordecai's answer to see if his explanation would prevail.

When Haman realized Mordecai would not kneel and bow down to him, he became angry. Believing a punishment for Mordecai as not enough, he decided to destroy all the Jews, Mordecai's people. In the first month of Nisan and the twelfth year of King Ahasuerus, Haman spoke to the king, telling him there are certain people living apart from others in the kingdom. He stated their laws differ from those of other people, and they refuse to obey the laws of the king. There is no evidence of this in the book with the exception of Mordecai's refusal to bow down before Haman. Haman expressed his belief that it was not proper for the king to tolerate the Jews.

In his conversation with the king, Haman strongly urged the king to issue a decree to destroy the Jews. If the king did this, he promised to donate 10,000 silver talents to the royal treasury. The king removed his royal signet from his finger and gave it to Haman, saying the silver was his to do with as he pleased. The royal signet was used to put the king's mark on a royal document.

Haman immediately summoned the scribes and dictated a royal decree to the royal satraps (governors). Dictating the decree in the name of the king and sealing the letters with the royal signet, he sent them to the royal provinces, telling them to destroy, kill, and annihilate all the Jews, young and old, women and children on a designated day.

In chapter B, the Greek addition to the book speaks of the contents of the letter. Sounding as though it comes from the king, the letter speaks of the king's desire to act fairly. He states he is determined to bring peace, tranquility, and safety for travelers to the farthest borders of his empire. He says Haman, who excels in discretion, who is outstanding for goodwill and resolute loyalty, and who is second in the kingdom only to him, brought some difficulties to his attention. Although the letter was actually dictated by Haman, it sounds as though the king is praising him. The letter declared there was one nation living among the people of the kingdom who are opposed to other people in the kingdom. Because of their disobedience to the king, they cause unity in the empire to be impossible.

Haman notes in the letter that this nation, meaning the Jews, lives by alien laws and is a danger to their government by striving to undermine the stability of the kingdom. All those indicated in this letter from Haman, who is in charge of the administration and a second father to all, shall be destroyed by the sword without any pity or mercy on the fourteenth day of the twelfth month, Adar, of the current year. The people, who acted with wickedness for a long period of time, shall have gone down to Hades by a violent death in a single day. This will leave the government completely stable and undisturbed in the future.

Chapter 3 says a copy of the decree was promulgated to all the people of Susa and elsewhere so they may be prepared for that day. The king and Haman sat down to drink, but Susa was thrown into frightening uncertainty.

## Lectio Divina

Spend 8 to 10 minutes in silent contemplation of the following passage:

Throughout history, the Jewish people often endured suffering and rejection. Unfortunately, prejudice and racism force people to make evil decisions against those they are oppressing. Haman is driven by his prejudice against the Jews. There is a slogan that says, "What goes around comes around." Evil people very often have to endure a type of suffering they inflict on others.

✠ *What can I learn from this passage?*

## Day 2: Esther and Mordecai Plead for Help (4, C, D, 5a)

When Mordecai learned about the decree from Haman, he tore his garments, put on sackcloth and ashes, and went through the city in mourning and wailing until he arrived at the royal gate that no one in sackcloth could enter. In each of the provinces reached by the king's decree and law, the Jews went into deep mourning, fasting, weeping, and lamenting wearing sackcloth and ashes.

When Esther's maids and eunuchs told her about Mordecai's mourning, she sent out garments for him to wear, but Mordecai refused to take off his sackcloth. Esther summoned Hathach, a eunuch placed at her service by the king, and commanded him to discover what caused Mordecai's anguish. When Hathach met with Mordecai, Mordecai explained the decree as well as the exact amount of silver Haman promised to pay to the royal treasury for the slaughter of the Jews. He gave Hathach a copy of the decree to show and explain to Esther. He told Hathach to instruct Esther to go to the king and intercede with him on behalf of her people.

Upon his return to Esther, Hathach told her what Mordecai said. Esther told Hathach to go to Mordecai and tell him of her dire situation. If anyone goes to the king without being summoned, that person will be put to death. Only if the king extends the golden scepter is one to go to him. The king has not summoned her for thirty days.

When Mordecai received Esther's words, he told her as a Jew, she was not to imagine she was safe in the king's palace. Even if she remains silent, relief and deliverance will come to the Jews from another source, but Esther and her father's house will perish. He speculated she may have become queen for a time like this. Esther sent word to Mordecai to go and assemble all the Jews who are in Susa and fast on her behalf, not eating or drinking, day and night for three days. She and her maids will do the same. Then, contrary to the law, she will go to the king. If she should perish, so be it. Mordecai did as Esther directed.

In chapter C, the Greek addition speaks of Mordecai's prayer. Mordecai prays to the Lord, whom he addresses as the King and Ruler of all, the Creator whom no one can resist. He tells the Lord he did not refuse to bow down before Haman out of arrogance or a desire for glory, saying he would have gladly kissed the soles of Haman's feet if it were for the salvation of Israel. Kissing the bottom of someone's foot was considered a highly humiliating action.

Mordecai refuses to bow down to anyone except the Lord. He begs the Lord, God of Abraham, to spare the Lord's people from their oppressors who regard them with deadly envy and seek to destroy the inheritance that was the Lord's from the beginning. He begs the Lord not to spurn the people the Lord redeemed from Egypt and to hear their prayer, have pity on them, and turn their mourning into feasting, so they may sing praise to the name of the Lord. All of Israel prayed with all their strength, since they were facing imminent death. Mordecai prays the Lord will not silence those who offer praise.

Queen Esther, filled with anguish, changed her splendid garments for garments of distress and mourning: "In place of her precious ointments she covered her head with dung and ashes. She afflicted her body severely and in place of her festive adornments, her tangled hair covered her" (C:13).

She prayed, saying the Lord alone was King, begging the Lord, her only help, to help her, for she is taking her life in her hand. She reviews what she heard about the Lord since her birth. She learned the Lord chose Israel from among the nations and her ancestors from among all their forebears. When they sinned, the Lord delivered them into the hands of their enemies because they worshiped the false gods. Now, the people have sworn to their gods to follow the decree ordering them to destroy the Lord's inheritance, to close the mouths of those who praise the Lord, and extinguish the glory of the Lord's house and altar.

She begs the Lord not to let their foes gloat over their ruin but to make an example of them. Wishing to make the Lord aware of her people's distress, she prays for courage. She prays for persuasive words in the presence of the lion (the king) so he will turn his heart against the enemies of the Jews. Praying Haman and his co-conspirators will perish, she begs the Lord to save and help her who has no one.

In her prayer, Esther tells the Lord she hates the pomp of the wicked and detests the bed of the uncircumcised foreigner. The Lord knows she is under constraint and abhors the crown she must wear in public. She claims she never ate at the table of Haman nor graced the banquet of the king or drank his wine. From the day she came to the king, she has had no joy except in the Lord. Begging the Lord to hear the voice of those in despair, she prays for deliverance from the wicked and from her fear.

In chapter D, the Greek addition speaks of Esther going before the king in great fear. She changed from her prayer garments and arrayed herself in her splendid attire. She went to the king with two maids, one to lean on and one to carry her train. Externally, she glowed with beauty and joy, but internally her heart was pounding in terror. She arrived before the king, who was arrayed in grandeur on his throne. His sudden look of anger caused Esther to stumble, turn pale, and faint. The Lord transformed the king's fury to tenderness. In great anxiety, he rushed to her, held her in his arms until she recovered, and comforted her with soothing words. He told her he was her brother and for her to have courage. Realizing she feared being put to death, he told her she shall not die. The law does not apply to the queen, but only to his subjects. He touched her neck with his scepter, embraced her, and told her to tell him whatever she wished.

Esther replied she saw him as an angel of God, and her heart was stunned at his majesty. She declares she saw his face as filled with mercy. When she said this, she fainted again, causing the king to become upset. The king's attendants attempted to revive her.

In chapter 5, the Hebrew segment begins where chapter 4 ended. It tells a different story of Esther going to the king.

Esther donned her royal garments and stood in the inner courtyard, gazing toward the royal palace. The king sat on his throne in the audience chamber, facing the palace doorway. When he spotted Queen Esther, she touched his heart and he extended the golden scepter toward her. She walked to him and touched the top of the scepter. Knowing she wanted to speak with him, he asked what she wanted. Because he loved her, he promised to give to her whatever she desires, even if it is half of his kingdom. Instead of making a request, she invites the king to come to a banquet she prepared and to bring Haman with him. The king ordered Haman, who was apparently in his presence, to quickly fulfill the wish of Esther.

## *Lectio Divina*

Spend 8 to 10 minutes in silent contemplation of the following passage:

The Greek addition in the Book of Esther shows a woman who is naturally frightened as she stands before the king and who faints in fear. She is offering her life for her people, but this does not make her feel any braver. Like many of the martyrs who died for Christ, she did not face death without fear, but she faced death despite her fear. Being willing to die for Christ does not necessarily take away the fear of torture or death.

✠ *What can I learn from this passage?*

---

## Day 3: Haman's Downfall (5:5b—8:2)

The king and Haman went to the banquet prepared by Esther. While the king was drinking wine, he repeated the words he spoke earlier, telling Esther he would give her whatever she wanted, even if it were half his kingdom. She asked for nothing except the presence of the king and Haman at a banquet she will prepare. She will make her request at that time.

Haman left the banquet quite pleased with himself. When at the royal gate he encountered Mordecai, who showed no fear and refused to rise to show him respect, he became furious. He controlled himself and went home, where he summoned his friends and wife. He recounted his abundant riches, the large number of his sons, and how the king placed him above the officials and royal servants. He spoke also about the invitation from Queen Esther to be her guest with the king the next day. He had to admit Mordecai ruined his joy. His wife and friends suggested he have a stake set up and in the morning impale Mordecai on it. Then, he can attend the banquet in good spirits. Liking this idea very much, he ordered the stake to be erected.

Chapter 6 returns to the king, who is unable to sleep. He asked the chronicle of notable events be brought to him. When the passage concerning Mordecai's report of the plot of the eunuchs to kill the king, he asked what was done for Mordecai, and the servants answered, "Nothing."

The king received word Haman had come to see him. When Haman came in, he asked him what should be done for a man the king wishes to reward.

---

Thinking the king was speaking about him, Haman answered the king should give his royal robe and horse to one of the noblest of the king's officials. He suggested the king allow the man to ride the king's horse in the public square of the city and have someone cry out before him that this is what is done for the man the king wishes to honor. The king agreed and told Haman to take the robe and horse as he has proposed and honor the Jew Mordecai, who is sitting at the royal gate, omitting nothing of what Haman suggested. Haman had to clothe Mordecai in the robe, put him on the horse, and walk in front of him, proclaiming this is what is done for the man the king wishes to honor.

Mordecai returned to the royal gate, while Haman hurried home grieving, with his head covered. When he told his family and friends what happened, they warned him if Mordecai, before whom he is beginning to fall, is of Jewish ancestry, he will not prevail against him but will be defeated by him. While they were conversing, the king's eunuchs arrived and hurried Haman off to the banquet prepared by Esther.

In chapter 7, the king and Haman again dined with Esther. As they were drinking, the king promised Esther he would grant her whatever she asks of him, even if it be half of his kingdom. Esther asks the king to spare her life and the life of her people, since it has been decreed they are to be destroyed, killed, and annihilated. If they were just to be sold into slavery, she told the king, she would not be troubling him. She fears the total annihilation of the Jewish people. King Ahasuerus asked Queen Esther to identify the man who dared to do this and give his location. She answered he is the wicked Haman. Fear of the king and queen seizes Haman.

The king left the banquet in anger and went to the garden of the palace. Since Haman knew the king had decided about his fate, he remained to beg Queen Esther for his life. When the king returned from the garden, he found Haman had thrown himself on the couch on which Esther was reclining. In his desperation, he was pleading with her for his life. The king exploded in anger, asking if Haman will also violate the queen while she is with the king in his own house. Haman turned his face away.

Harbona, one of the eunuchs who attended the king, told the king about the stake fifty cubits high on which Haman intended to impale Mordecai. The king ordered the eunuch to impale Haman on it. When they impaled him, the king's anger was abated.

In chapter 8, King Ahasuerus gave the house of Haman to Queen Esther and admitted Mordecai into his presence once Esther revealed his relationship to her. The king removed the signet ring he took from Haman and gave it to Mordecai. Esther put Mordecai in charge of the house of Haman.

### *Lectio Divina*

Spend 8 to 10 minutes in silent contemplation of the following passage:

Haman's anger with Mordecai led him to make a foolish decision that later led to his downfall. He thought he was powerful and in control, but in reality, his pride, arrogance, and anger controlled him. Whenever people consider themselves better than others, they do not control their feelings. Their feelings control and damage them.

✠ *What can I learn from this passage?*

## Day 4: The Jewish Feast and the Feast of Purim (8:3–12, E, 8:13–17, 9:1–23)

Queen Esther tearfully begged the king to cancel the damage done by Haman. The king gave her authority equal to Haman. Since Haman had been impaled and she received the house of Haman, she may in turn write in the king's name and seal a decree with the signet ring. The people must obey it.

Esther and Mordecai called in the scribes, who then wrote what Mordecai dictated. He sent the decree with the royal signet to the people with couriers riding royal steeds. The king authorized the Jews to defend themselves, to destroy, kill, and annihilate every armed group of any nation attacking them and to seize their goods. According to the custom of the Medes and Persians, promulgated laws cannot be revoked. Instead of revoking the law, the king gave the Jews the right to defend themselves without breaking the law.

In chapter E, the added Greek manuscript offers a copy of the letter dictated by Mordecai and sent as coming from the king. The letter states many who were showered with the generosity of their patrons had become ambitious, not only seeking to harm the subjects of the kingdom but also their benefactor, meaning the king. In their arrogance, they believe they will escape the judgment of the all-seeing God.

Those entrusted with the administration of affairs became accomplices in shedding innocent blood and committing lasting harm by slandering the goodwill of rulers. The truth of such a statement can be verified in ancient stories handed down, but even more when the people consider the iniquity committed in their midst. Now, the king must provide for the future, rendering the kingdom peaceful for all people.

The letter names Haman, a Macedonian, who was not of Persian blood and very different from the king in generosity. He benefited a great deal from the goodwill the king has for all people and was proclaimed "our father," before whom everyone was to bow down. Unable to control his arrogance, he demanded the death of Mordecai, the savior and constant benefactor, and Esther, the king's blameless cohort, along with their whole nation.

The letter declares the Jews who were doomed to extinction by Haman are governed by very just laws and are the children of the Most High God. The people are to ignore the letter sent by Haman who has been impaled with his whole household. The Jews may follow their own law and defend themselves against those who attack them. Therefore, the Jews must celebrate this memorable day among their designated feasts with all rejoicing as a celebration of deliverance and for those who plot against the Jews a day of destruction. Every place ignoring this decree will be ruthlessly destroyed with fire and sword and left desolate. The Jews name this feast as the feast of Purim.

With the end of the letter, the text returns to chapter 8. A copy of the letter was promulgated among all the people so the Jews can be prepared to avenge themselves against their enemies. Mordecai was clothed in a royal robe of violet and white cotton, with a crown of gold and mantle of fine crimson linen. The people of Susa cried out in joy, and for the Jews in every province it was a day of joy and triumph. Many of the people identified themselves as Jews to avoid punishment.

In chapter 9, when the day arrived for the slaughter of the Jews, the Jews overpowered those who sought to do them harm. The officials of the king joined with the Jews in fighting against the enemy out of fear of Mordecai, who was continually growing in power. In the royal precinct of Susa alone, the Jews killed 500 people, among them the ten sons of Haman. The Jews did not plunder the goods of those they killed.

When the king reported to Esther about the death of the 500 people and the ten sons of Haman, he again told her she could request whatever she wished. She requested the decree be extended another day and the bodies of the ten sons of Haman impaled on stakes. The king granted her request and the Jews killed 300 more on the day the ten sons of Haman were impaled. Again, they did not plunder.

On the fourteenth day of the month, the Jews rested and celebrated the day as a day of rejoicing and feasting and they did the same on the fifteenth day. Mordecai ordered the Jews to celebrate the feast every year with joyful banqueting, exchanging gifts, and offering gifts to the poor.

### *Lectio Divina*

Spend 8 to 10 minutes in silent contemplation of the following passage:

Life has its ups and downs. Mordecai, Esther, and the Jewish people lived comfortably until Haman threatened their existence. They went through a period of pain. In the end, however, they were freed from the threat of annihilation, and Jews throughout the ages celebrate their salvation by celebrating the feast of Purim. Jesus experienced a day when people cheered for him as he entered Jerusalem in triumph. After his Palm Sunday, Jesus encountered his Good Friday, and finally his joyful Easter Sunday, a day of resurrection. Life is like that, with many minor deaths and resurrections, as the Jews in the Book of Esther showed us.

✠ *What can I learn from this passage?*

## Day 5: Epilogue—The Rise of Mordecai (9:24—10, F)

The end of chapter 9 summarizes the events that occurred in the Book of Esther leading up to the celebration of the feast of Purim. Haman planned to destroy the Jews and cast a lot (pur) for the time of their destruction. When the king learned of the plot, he ordered Haman and his ten sons impaled on stakes. The Jews established a yearly feast of celebration on these two days just as Mordecai and Queen Esther decreed in a letter. The days of Purim were never to be forgotten by the descendants of the Jews.

Chapter 10 states the authority and courage of Mordecai are recorded in the chronicles of the kings of Media and Persia. The Jew Mordecai, who sought the good of his people and spoke out for their welfare, became next in rank to the king and was renowned among the Jews and his kindred.

In F, the Greek edition adds Mordecai's explanation of the dream he had at the beginning of the book. In his dream there was a time of turmoil. He applies the stream that became a river in his dream as a symbol of Esther. The two dragons in the dream refer to Haman (the bad dragon) and Mordecai (the good dragon). The nations ready to fight against the just nation were those assembled to destroy the Jews from the face of the earth. The lowly nation of the just, the Jews, cried out to God and were saved. The sun and light broke through when the Jews found salvation in the signs and wonders of the Lord.

A postscript meant to date the letter simply indicates it may have been written between 116 BC and 48 BC. It was written in the fourth year of Ptolemy and Cleopatra. There were several Greek kings reigning in Egypt with the designation of Ptolemy who had wives named Cleopatra. Ptolemy identifies Lysimachus of the community of Jerusalem as the translator of the book.

### Lectio Divina

Spend 8 to 10 minutes in silent contemplation of the following passage:

Mordecai was a faithful and prayerful Jew who had to endure much, but he still defended his faith in God and could speak with joy about the presence of God. Love of God provides people with a new power in the midst of pain and joy. Faith and love of God should bring joy. Pope Francis, in an exhortation, wrote that Christians should not look like they are returning from a funeral.

✠ *What can I learn from this passage?*

## Review Questions

1. What is the meaning of Mordecai's dream?
2. How did Esther become queen?
3. What was Haman's plot against the Jews?
4. Why is the feast of Purim so important for the Jews?

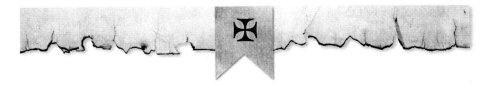

# The Book of First Maccabees (I)

## 1 MACCABEES 1—9:22

*Then Judas and his brothers and the entire assembly of Israel decreed that every year for eight days, from the twenty-fifth day of the month Kislev, the days of the dedication of the altar should be observed with joy and gladness on the anniversary (4:59).*

**Opening Prayer** (SEE PAGE 15)

## Context

**Part 1: 1 Maccabees (1—2:14)** The Book of 1 Maccabees receives its name from the hero of the book, Judas Maccabeus. The book begins with the story of the oppression of Antiochus IV of the people of Judea that began in the second century before Christ. The book itself was probably written in Hebrew around the year 100 BC, although being lost over time, the later Greek translation became the basis for the Biblical text. The books of 1 and 2 Maccabees are not found in the Hebrew or Protestant Bibles but are in the Catholic Bible and are considered to be inspired.

Mattathias kills a Jew who came forward to offer sacrifice on the altar in Modein and flees with his five sons and many of the faithful Israelites.

**Part 2: 1 Maccabees (2:15—9:22)** The sons of Mattathias continue to fight against Antiochus IV, who strives to force the Greek culture and gods on the Israelites. Judas becomes a major leader in Judea who leads the people to a number of successful battles. When he dies, the people view him as their savior.

## PART 1: GROUP STUDY (1 MACCABEES 1—2:14)

Read aloud 1 Maccabees 1—2:14.

### 1:1–40 Religious Persecution

When Alexander the Great defeated Darius, king of the Persians and the Medes, in 331 BC, he captured the Persian Empire. Since Jerusalem and Judea (a new name for Judah) were part of the Persian Empire, they now belonged to Alexander's Greek Empire. After a series of battles, captured fortresses, and the murder of many kings, Alexander the Great died in 323 BC at thirty-two.

The Book of 1 Maccabees states Alexander divided his kingdom among his generals while he was still alive. In reality, his generals fought battles to gain portions of the kingdom. By 281 BC, Alexander's kingdom consisted of three separate kingdoms, Ptolemy in Egypt, Seleucus I in Syria, and Cassander in Macedonia and Greece. Since Palestine was between Egypt and Syria, the greatest concern for the people of Palestine was Ptolemy in Egypt and the Seleucids in Syria. The Ptolemy kingdom and the Seleucid kingdom fought several wars over control of Palestine. In 198 BC, King Antiochus III, the Seleucid, conquered Israel and Jerusalem and allowed the Jews to continue their religious practices with their own high priest.

After losing a battle to the Romans, King Antiochus III, who had to pay tribute to Rome, was in dire need of finances. In an attempt to raid a Babylonian temple for plunder, King Antiochus III was killed. After the death of Antiochus III, his oldest son, Seleucus IV, succeeded him. He was eventually assassinated by a usurper who was also killed, leaving the throne for Antiochus IV, a third son of Antiochus III, who was not in direct line for becoming king, but with the help of a co-conspirator, took it for himself. He became king in September, 175 BC. He was referred to as Antiochus Epiphanies, which means "God Manifest." Because of his strange and often cruel manner of acting, he became known among many as Antiochus Epimanes, which means "mad man."

Since the time of Alexander, two factions existed among the Jews in Judea, the traditionalist faction consisting of Jews who clung desperately to their God and their Jewish traditions, and the Hellenized faction favoring the Greek culture, language, and gods. These latter were the "lawless Jews," a name they received from their opponents because they sinned against the Torah. The lawless Jews sided with the king who authorized them to introduce the Greek culture.

In accord with the Gentile custom, the lawless Jews abandoned the covenant by building a gymnasium and removing their circumcision by a surgical procedure. The gymnasium was the place used for sports and intellectual learning. The reason they had to hide their circumcision was due to the practice of athletics taking place in the nude.

Antiochus IV fought against the Ptolemy power in Egypt to gain total power over Palestine. Returning from Egypt after a victory over the Ptolemy kingdom, Antiochus IV, in need of funds, raided Jerusalem, and ransacked and plundered all the gold from the Temple, took the golden altar, the vessels, and the ornamentation. In the process he killed many Israelites before returning to his own country.

In light of the ransacking of the Temple and the killing of the people, the author presents a lamentation. He sings of young women and men and a bridegroom and bride languishing in grief. Shame covered the house of Jacob (Israel).

Two years after Antiochus ravaged the Temple, he sent the Mysian commander to the cities of Judah. He came to Jerusalem with a powerful army. In 2 Maccabees, the author identifies the Mysian commander as Apollonius, commander of the Mysians who were mercenaries from Asia Minor. He lured the people with deceptive words of peace, and they believed him. Once he gained their confidence, he suddenly attacked and killed many of the people, plundering and destroying the city with fire, and seizing the men, women, and animals.

After demolishing the city, the Mysians built up the city of David with high, firm walls and towers, making it an unyielding fortress. Gentiles and the lawless Jews, who supported the Seleucids, inhabited the city and stockpiled weapons and provisions they had plundered from Jerusalem.

The author of 1 Maccabees inserts a lament at this point, singing sadly about the stronghold as a place of ambush for the people in the sanctuary, forcing the inhabitants of Jerusalem to flee from the city and making the city an abode of strangers and a land of desolation. When the people should be feasting, instead they mourn. Her (Jerusalem's) dishonor became as great as her previous glory.

### 1:41—2:14 Greek Culture Ordered

In an attempt to force the Greek culture on the Jews, the king sent letters by messenger to Jerusalem and the cities of Judah, ordering them to follow foreign customs that forbade burnt offerings, sacrifices, libations in the Temple, and honoring the Sabbath and feast days. He ordered them to desecrate the sanctuary and sacred ministers and build pagan altars, temples, and shrines to sacrifice swine and unclean animals. To carry out his orders, Antiochus sent in inspectors. Those who refused to follow the Law were forced into hiding wherever they could find places of refuge.

On December 6, 167 BC, the king challenged the faithful Israelites in a dramatic fashion, erecting the desolating abomination upon the altar of burnt offering and building pagan altars in the surrounding cities of Judah. The abomination seems to refer to an image of a god the people worshiped or an altar for worship of such a god. He ordered the people to burn any scrolls of the Law they found. The scrolls of the Law refer to the Torah, the first five books of the Bible or segments of it. Those found with a copy of the scrolls or observing the Law were condemned to horrible forms of death. Also condemned to death were women, who had their sons circumcised, and those who circumcised them were killed. Their babies were hanged. Many faithful Israelites planned to die rather than eat unclean food.

Mattathias, a father of five sons—John, Simon, Judas, Eleazar, and Jonathan—left Jerusalem for his hometown of Modein, which was about twenty miles northwest of Jerusalem. Mattathias proclaimed a lament when he saw the sacrileges taking place in Judah and Jerusalem. When he observed the wreckage of his people, he lamented the day he was born. He witnessed the ruin of the holy city, the foreigners in the dishonored Temple, the murder of infants in the streets, and the murder of its youth. The nation, once free, had become a slave and the beauty and glory of its sanctuary ravaged by the Gentiles. Mattathias and his sons put on sackcloth and mourned bitterly.

## *Review Questions*

1. Who is Antiochus Epiphanes and what did he do to God's Temple?
2. How did Antiochus seek to impose the Greek culture on the people?
3. Who were the lawless ones?

### **Closing Prayer** (SEE PAGE 15)

Pray the closing prayer now or after *lectio divina*.

### *Lectio Divina* (SEE PAGE 8)

Relax your body and maintain a posture of prayer (back straight, eyes shut, feet flat on the floor). This exercise can take as long as you want, but in the context of this Bible study, 10 to 20 minutes should be sufficient.

The meditations that follow are provided only to help group participants use this prayer form, but note that *lectio* is intended to bring one to a place of prayerful contemplation where the Word of God speaks to the hearer from his or her heart. (See page 8 for further instruction.)

### *Religious Persecution (1:1–40)*

The people had an opportunity to save themselves if they would reject their Mosaic Law and accept the Greek culture, which involved rejecting circumcision and worshiping a false god. For many of the Jews, the ways of the Gentile Greeks were far more alluring and pleasurable than Judaism. In the world today, many Christians accept torture or death rather than abandon their faith, while others, in countries where they have the opportunity to worship freely, abandon their faith for the allurements of a more pleasurable or easier life. The challenge of remaining faithful is present in every age.

✠ *What can I learn from this passage?*

### Greek Culture Ordered (1:41—2:14)

When Mattathias witnesses the apostasy of his people, he laments the day he was born. God, however, needs people in the world like Mattathias to give an example of courage and faithfulness to the law of God. Paul the Apostle lived in a world filled with sin and longed to be with God, but he knew how important he was to God in the world. He writes, "I long to depart this life and be with Christ, [for] that is far better. Yet that I remain [in] the flesh is more necessary for your benefit" (Philippians 1:23–24). The Lord needs us to give the world an example of the life of people dedicated to the love of God.

✠ *What can I learn from this passage?*

---

## PART 2: INDIVIDUAL STUDY (1 MACCABEES 2:15—9:22)

---

### Day 1: Mattathias' Revolt (2:15—3)

The envoys of the king, those enforcing apostasy, came to Modein. Conscious of the importance of Mattathias in the eyes of the people, they attempted to lure him to follow the ways of those in Jerusalem who followed the way of the Gentiles. They knew if Mattathias accepted the decree of the king, others would follow. Mattathias shouted loud enough for all to hear, saying he and his sons would not obey the king's order by departing from their religion.

When he finished speaking, a Jew came forward and offered sacrifice on the altar of Modein according to the king's order. When Mattathias saw this, he became furious and killed the man on the altar. He then killed the messenger and tore down the altar. In doing this, he showed his zeal just as Phinehas, Aaron's grandson, did when he killed the Israelite who brought a Midianite woman into his tent (see Numbers 25:6–15). Mattathias called out for those who were zealous for the Law to follow him. He and his sons abandoned their possessions and left the city.

Many who sought to remain faithful to the covenant went out into the wilderness, to the mountain country south of Jerusalem near the Dead Sea. When the soldiers of the king learned they had gone into the wilderness, they went out after them, planning to attack them on the Sabbath when the faithful people would most likely not strike back. Because they firmly remained faithful to keeping the Sabbath according to Mosaic Law and would not fight, they did nothing to protect themselves when they were attacked. As a result, 1,000 men with their wives, children, and animals were killed.

Mattathias realized those faithful to the Law would have to fight on the Sabbath if they were to survive. A group of Israelite warriors faithful to the Law, known as the Hasideans, joined them. The word "Hasidim" in Hebrew means "pious ones." Concerned mainly about the Law and not political victories, they would later reject the revolt of the Maccabees. Other Israelites, who were fleeing from the Gentile soldiers, also joined them. Mattathias and his sons formed an army and killed the lawless and the survivors who attempted to flee to the Gentiles for safety. A priority for Mattathias and his followers was the destruction of the lawless Jews.

When Mattathias was dying, he urged each son to be zealous and offer his life to the Lord. He recalls in poetic form the deeds of their ancestors. He recalls the just deeds of Abraham, who was willing to sacrifice his son to God, the distress of Joseph in Egypt when he was falsely accused, the deed of Phinehas in killing a sinful Israelite, the leadership of Joshua for leading the people into the Promised Land, the loyalty of Caleb in his support for Joshua, the kingship of David for his loyalty, the blessings of Elijah for his zeal for the Law, the bravery of Hananiah, Azariah, and Mishael for their faithfulness to the Lord, and the valor of Daniel for his trust in the Lord. He tells his sons not to fear the words of sinners whose glory ends in corruption. They are exalted today and forgotten tomorrow. When they return to the dust, their schemes are forgotten while those who live by the Law will be honored.

Mattathias appointed Simon as the wise counselor for the faithful Israelites and Judas as the leader of their army. He urged them to avenge themselves against the Gentiles. Mattathias died in 166 BC.

In chapter 3, Mattathias' son, Judas, becomes the central character of the book. He is called Maccabeus, which means "the hammer." Although his name applies only to him, it is his title which gives the books of Maccabees their name. Judas has not yet begun to lead the people, but the song views him as having defended the people with valor. Through his leadership, the glory of the people became renowned. He put on a breastplate like a giant, fought battles, protected the camp with his sword, pursued the lawless, and destroyed those who distressed his people. The song declares the lawless and evildoers feared him. The Israelites rejoiced at his deeds and his memory is blessed forever. He destroyed the unfaithful in the cities of Judah and turned oppression away from Israel. Because he saved those who were perishing, he is renowned to the ends of the earth.

Then Apollonius gathered the Gentiles and a large army from Samaria to fight against Israel. When Judas learned of Apollonius' plans, Judas fought against him, killing him and many of his troops and sending the Gentiles who survived fleeing. Judas took the sword of Apollonius and used it in battle for the rest of his life.

Seron, a commander of the Syrian army, believed he could make a name for himself by defeating Judas in battle. Judas chose only a few soldiers to fight against Seron. When Judas' small army saw Seron's large number of troops coming against them, they asked Judas how so few can fight against so many. Judas' faith offered encouragement. He said their strength came from heaven, meaning it came from the Lord. Many pious Jews would use the word "heaven" in place of the name of God.

Judas told his troops they were fighting for their life and laws. He trusted the Lord would help crush the enemy. After speaking, he led a charge against Seron and his army, routing them and killing 800 of their men. The survivors fled to the land of the Philistines. Judas' fame spread to the king and the Gentiles, who now began to fear him.

When King Antiochus heard the reports concerning Judas and his army, he gave his soldiers a year's pay and commanded them to be prepared for anything. His rash move depleted his treasury. Since the income from the province was not as generous as in the past, he decided he would go to Persia with half his army to raise a large sum of money by levying tribute (taxes for protection) on these provinces and would send the other half of his army against the Jews.

Antiochus left a nobleman of royal descent named Lysias in charge of his territory from the Euphrates River to the borders of Egypt. Instructing Lysias to send forces against the Israelites in Jerusalem and Judea and wipe their memory from the face of the earth, he took his half of the forces and left for his mission.

Lysias chose three powerful men—Ptolemy, Nicanor, and Gorgias—to lead 40,000 foot soldiers and 7,000 cavalry to ravage the land of Judah. The army camped at Emmaus (not the Emmaus in the Gospel story found in Luke 24:13–35). When the merchants in the area heard of the army and its intentions, they brought silver and gold to buy the captured Israelites as slaves. Other forces joined the Greek military in preparation for the battle.

When Judas heard of the intention of Antiochus' army to wipe out the Israelites, he and his men prayed a lament. They lamented the desolation of Jerusalem, the profanation of the Temple, the infestation of the land with Gentiles, and the loss of joy and music among the people. They went to Mizpah (a place for prayer), where they fasted, wore sackcloth, covered their heads with ashes, and tore their garments. Unlike the Gentiles who conferred with false gods, they consulted the Law to read the directions of the Lord.

They asked God what they should do with the vestments, the first fruits, and tithes, and they presented the nazarites, faithful men who bound themselves to the Lord through vows. Without the Temple, they did not know what to do with these offerings. They asked the Lord to help them against the Gentiles.

Following the Law in Deuteronomy, Judas sent home those who were building a house, newly married, planting a vineyard, and those who were afraid (see Deuteronomy 20:5–8). Judas prepared his army to fight in the morning, saying it is better to die than to witness the evil imposed on their nation. He trusts himself to the Lord, saying whatever is willed in heaven will take place.

### Lectio Divina

Spend 8 to 10 minutes in silent contemplation of the following passage:

When Mattathias died, many people may have wondered how the Lord would replace such a zealous leader. The Lord sent Judas Maccabeus to help the people. For people of faith, God provides helpful leaders. When a well-loved leader dies (such as the pope), people wonder if the Lord will send a leader like the one who died. The Lord responds to the prayers of people of faith.

✠ *What can I learn from this passage?*

## Day 2: Victory Over Gorgias (4—5)

While Judas and his men rested, the Gentile warrior Gorgias took 5,000 infantry and 1,000 cavalry to lead a surprise attack against Judas. Having been alerted of the attack, Judas slipped his troops out of the camp and led them against the Gentiles' camp at Emmaus while Gorgias' forces were away. When Gorgias' men arrived at the Israelite camp, they found it empty and believed the Israelites fled in fear into the mountains. The forces of Gorgias charged into the mountains thinking they would crush the fleeing Israelites.

In the meanwhile, Judas led his forces against the army of the Gentiles, who were well-equipped and experienced for battle. Recalling for his forces how the Lord saved the Israelite ancestors at the Red Sea when the Egyptians pursued them, he encouraged his men not to fear. He urged them to cry to heaven in hopes the Lord will remember the covenant and destroy the Gentile army before them. When the Lord answers their prayers, the army will then know there is one who redeems and saves Israel. Judas then led his army into battle and killed 3,000 Gentile warriors, and the remainder of the Gentiles fled. Judas told his men not to take plunder at this time, since they still had to face Gorgias' army.

When Gorgias' detachment came to the top of the mountain above the plain, they saw their camp burning and Judas' army lined up for battle in the front of it. Surprised at the destruction of the camp, the troops panicked and fled back to their own land. Judas and his men returned to the camp and plundered it. They returned home glorifying heaven (God) and singing hymns of praise.

When Lysias heard about the defeat of the army, he was deeply disheartened. The following year, he gathered a force of 60,000 specially chosen men and 5,000 cavalry to march against Judas. When Judas saw the strength of the army coming against him, he prayed to the Lord, who protected and helped David and Jonathan, the Son of Saul, and his armor-bearer (see 1 Samuel 17:48–58). He prayed the Lord would shame these forces and fill them with fear and cowardice. In begging the Lord to allow his men, who love the Lord, to cut down the Gentiles, he sang the Lord's praises. In the battle, Judas' army killed about 5,000 men of Lysias' army. Lysias returned to Antioch and began to recruit mercenaries so he could return against Judas with a larger army.

Judas and his whole army went up to Mount Zion, where they found the sanctuary desolate, the altar desecrated, the gates burnt, and the priests' chambers destroyed. They put on clothing for mourning and cried out to heaven. Since a few Gentiles still remained in their fortification, Judas sent men to attack them. He then chose priests dedicated to the Law to set about purifying the sanctuary (the whole Temple area).

Because the altar had been desecrated with Gentile offerings, the priests decided to destroy the old altar and build a new one. They set the old stones on the Temple mount until a prophet could determine what to do with them. Following the directives of Exodus 20:25, they built a new altar from uncut stones. They made new furnishings and vessels for Temple worship, burned incense on the altar, lighted the lamps, put loaves on the table, and hung up the curtains. On December 14, 164 BC, they rededicated the altar on the anniversary of the day the Gentiles desecrated it and celebrated with songs, harps, lyres, and cymbals. The people prostrated themselves in adoration and praise of heaven (the Lord) who made them successful.

For eight days, the people celebrated the dedication of the altar, offered burnt sacrifices of deliverance and praise, and finished repairing and adorning the sanctuary. Judas, his brothers, and the entire assembly decreed the anniversary of the days of dedication of the altar should be observed with joy for eight days, beginning with the twenty-fifth day of the month of Kislev. The Jewish people celebrate this event each year as the feast of Hanukkah, also known as the feast of Dedication. The Israelites fortified Mount Zion with high walls and strong towers. Judas appointed a garrison to protect it.

Chapter 5 presents a series of victories for Judas Maccabeus, making him feared among the Gentiles and more honored among the Israelites. The events took place during the year 163 BC. The rebuilding of the altar and restoration of the sanctuary inflamed the Gentile nations, whose people began to kill the Israelites in their midst, hoping to destroy them completely. Because the Edomites (descendants of Esau, the brother of Jacob) were blockading the trade routes of Israel, Judas crushed them. He attacked another nation, known as the Baeanites, who were also ambushing the Israelites along the roads. When they took refuge in their towers, Judas put them under the ban, which meant he would kill every one of them. He burned down their towers with all those in it.

After this, Judas crossed over to the Ammonites, where he encountered a strong army and a large number of people with a leader named Timothy. Timothy appears to have been a local leader. Judas defeated the Ammonites in several battles. During his return to Judea, he seized a town named Jazer.

When the Gentiles in Gilead prepared to demolish the Israelites who lived in their territory, the Israelites fled to a stronghold name Dathema, east of the Jordan. They sent a letter to Judas and his brothers saying the Gentiles were assembling to destroy them and seize their stronghold. They said Timothy was their leader. They begged Judas and his brothers to come and help them. They reported all their kindred in the territory of the Tobiads were killed and their wives, children, and property captured. The Gentiles slaughtered about 1,000 men there. The Tobiads were a well-known family that settled east of the Jordan.

At the same time, other messengers with their garments torn came to Judas saying the inhabitants of the Ptolemais, Tyre, and Sidon, and all the Gentiles had joined together to destroy them. Confronted with the troubles of their kindred in two different areas, Judas told his brother, Simon, to choose some men and go to Galilee while he and Jonathan went to Gilead.

When he left, he appointed a man named Joseph with the rest of the army in Judea to guard it. He commanded them not to join in battle against the Gentiles until his return. Simon led his army against the Gentiles and killed about 3,000 people. He gathered the spoils of his victories and led a group of Jewish men, women, children, and all they possessed to Judea.

Judas and his brother, Jonathan, led the army for three days through the wilderness. During their journey, they met some Nabateans, an Arab tribe of merchants, who welcomed them peacefully and informed them about their kindred in Gilead. They told them many were shut up in a fortification in Bozrah and other fortified cities. Judas changed direction. When he reached Bozrah, he killed a large number of the Gentiles and captured the city, burning it to the ground. He led his army toward a Jewish stronghold, and when he saw a large multitude of Timothy's army storming the wall and attempting to capture the city, he came up behind them with the loud blare of trumpets.

When Timothy's army realized it was Judas Maccabeus, they fled. Judas' army killed about 8,000 Gentiles and went on to defeat Timothy's forces.

Judas sent spies to Timothy's camp, who reported all the Gentiles in the surrounding area and some hired Arabs had joined Timothy. The army of Judas marched against Timothy's forces. A wadi with flowing water separated Judas' warriors from those of Timothy. Timothy told his army they would not be able to overcome Judas if he crossed the wadi, but if he shows fear and camps on the other side of the river, they will cross over and defeat him. Judas ordered his men not to allow anyone to set up camp. They must fight. Judas' troops crossed the wadi and annihilated the Gentile force. Those remaining threw aside their arms and fled into the temple of a Syrian goddess. Judas' troops captured the city and burnt the temple and all who were in it.

Judas gathered all the Israelites of Gilead together with their wives, children, and possessions, and led them back toward the land of Judah. When they reached a strongly fortified city named Ephron, they found it impossible to go around it, so they sought permission to go through it, but the people of the city blocked the gates with stones. As a result, Judas captured the city after assaulting it day and night. He killed all the men, leveled the city, plundered it, and passed through it over the dead bodies. As he continued his journey, he kept gathering stragglers and offering encouragement to the people right up to the day they joyfully reached Mount Zion.

When Joseph and Azariah heard about the brave deeds of Judas, Jonathan, and Simon, they wanted to gain some renown for themselves. They marched against a city named Jamnia, but Gorgias engaged them in battle, pursued them to the frontiers of Judea, and killed 2,000 Israelites. The defeat disheartened the people, who were ashamed because they did not obey Judas' orders.

Jews and Gentiles alike praised the name of Judas and his brothers for their valiant deeds. Judas successfully attacked the Edomites and in his conflicts destroyed the carved images of the people's gods and plundered their cities.

## Lectio Divina

Spend 8 to 10 minutes in silent contemplation of the following passage:

When the Jewish people celebrate feasts such as Hanukkah, they recall what happened to them in the past and are reminded that God remains active in their life today. Religious celebrations in all religions are meant to remind us of God's presence, not only in past events but also in the present. The feasts do not say, "God was once with us," but instead say, "God is with us now."

✠ *What can I learn from this passage?*

## Day 3: Victories Over Hostile Neighbors (6—7)

Antiochus IV heard there was a city in Persia named Elam that possessed great wealth and an abundance of silver and gold helmets, breastplates, and weapons once belonging to the army of Alexander the Great. Since he was in dire need of funds, he intended to capture and loot the city. The townspeople, however, learned of his plan and successfully warded off the king's attack.

While Antiochus was in Persia, a messenger told him of the defeat of Lysias in Judah, adding the Jews became more powerful due to the arms and wealth they captured from Lysias' army. The messenger informed him about the Jews tearing down the altar of abomination in the Temple and their construction of high walls around the sanctuary area and the city of Beth-zur. Upon hearing this news, Antiochus became sick and bedridden with grief. Believing he was going to die, he lamented the anxiety he felt when he recalled his evil deeds in sacking the Temple in Jerusalem. His remorse may be the author's addition to show Antiochus' sickness and death resulted from his sacking of the Temple rather than his defeat in the east.

Knowing he was going to die, he summoned Philip, one of his friends, and gave him his diadem, his robe, and his signet ring so he could bring up his son, Antiochus, to be king. He died in 164 or 163 BC. When Lysias in Antioch learned Antiochus IV had died, he set up the king's son, Antiochus, to be king and gave him the title "eupator," which means "of a good father."

In Jerusalem, the Gentiles from "the citadel" were harassing the Israelites in the sanctuary, so Judas seized the secure fortress, but some of the trapped

Gentiles escaped along with some renegade Israelites. (A citadel was a fortification in a city or part of a city, sometimes with a tower in the middle. See
1 Maccabees 1:33.) The defecting Israelites went to King Antiochus V and
asked how long he would wait before avenging their kindred being killed by
Judas and his army. They would actually be complaining to Lysias, who was
acting in the name of the child-king. The Gentiles and defectors complained
the army of Judas has been attacking them throughout the land, killing
their kindred who were defecting to the Greeks. They informed the king of
the attack on the fortress in Jerusalem and warned the army had also fortified the sanctuary and Beth-zur. They warned the king the army will do far
worse if it is not stopped.

The king, under the direction of Lysias, gathered together all his army officers and cavalry commanders. Mercenaries joined them, and they went into
battle with 100,000 foot soldiers, 20,000 cavalry, and thirty-two elephants
trained for war. For many days, they fought at Beth-zur. They constructed
siege engines, but those in the city slipped away from the city and burned
the siege engines.

Judas marched out to Beth-zechariah, which was south of Jerusalem and
six miles north of Beth-zur. The king's army made the elephants drunk with
wine and mulberries to get them ready to fight. The elephants led with 1,000
men in military gear alongside. Each elephant carried a strong wooden tower
fastened by a harness with three soldiers fighting from the tower. The army
moved with military precision, with the army marching close together and
the cavalry spread out from the ranks of the army.

In the battle, Judas' troops managed to kill 600 of the king's army. Eleazar,
Judas' brother, noticed one elephant was bigger than the others. Believing
the king would be in its tower, he rushed toward it, killing the enemy as he
ran. Getting under the elephant, he stabbed and killed it. The elephant fell
dead on top of Eleazar and killed him. Judas and his army had to retreat from
the king's powerful army.

Some of the king's army then set up camps in Judea and at Mount Zion with
the intention of attacking Jerusalem. The king made peace with the people
of Beth-zur. The people, lacking food, evacuated the city. It was a Sabbath
year, which meant a year when sowing and reaping the land was forbidden

by the Mosaic Law (Exodus 23:10–11). With no harvest, the people could not replenish their provisions.

The king then laid siege to the sanctuary in Jerusalem, using platforms, siege engines, fire-throwers, catapults, and mechanical bows for shooting arrows and projectiles. The defenders set up siege engines and fought valiantly, but due to the Sabbath year and the lack of supplies, only a few men remained in the sanctuary while the rest scattered.

When Lysias learned in Judea that Philip, the friend of Antiochus chosen to raise his son, had returned from Persia and Media with the army of Antiochus IV and was seeking to take over the government, he was anxious to return to Antioch. The king made peace with the Jews, solidifying his offer of peace with an oath. The Jews evacuated the fortification on Mount Zion, but when the king entered the city and saw how strong its fortifications were, he broke his oath and ordered the wall to be torn down. He then left for Antioch.

In chapter 7, Demetrius, the son of Seleucus and the rightful heir to the throne, escaped in 161 BC from Rome where his father had sent him as a hostage in exchange for his brother, Antiochus IV. Demetrius returned to Syria as its proper ruler. When Demetrius' soldiers seized the child Antiochus V and Lysias, he refused to see their faces and had them put to death.

All the lawless then joined Demetrius. Knowing Judas was killing those who defected, they urged the king to send an army with a man he could trust to destroy Judas and his army. The king sent a man named Bacchides, who was faithful to the king. He sent with him Alcimus, whom he named as high priest. When they arrived in the land of Judah, they attempted to lure Judas and his brothers to agree to misleading terms of peace. Upon seeing the army Bacchides brought with him, Judas and his army were not deceived. They refused to speak of peace.

In the meanwhile, a group of scribes from among the Hasideans sought peace, believing they could trust a priest in the line of Aaron, who traveled with the Bacchides' army. Alcimus, however, had sixty of them arrested and, in one day, killed them all. Bacchides turned on those who defected to him and ordered them killed and their bodies thrown into the cistern. He left Alcimus in charge of the province with an adequate amount of troops. Judas' army continued to travel throughout Judea, taking revenge on those who deserted.

When Alcimus realized Judas and his companions were becoming stronger, he returned to the king and accused them of grave offenses.

The king sent Nicanor, one of his officers, with orders to annihilate the people. Arriving in Jerusalem with a large force, Nicanor sent a message to Judas, saying he would come with a few men to negotiate a peace settlement. Judas, knowing the peace offer was a sham, refused to meet with him. As a result, Nicanor and his force went to battle Judas' army. Judas' warriors killed about 500 men, and the remainder fled.

Gathering his forces, Nicanor marched up to Mount Zion. Some priests and elders came from the sanctuary to welcome him peacefully and show him the burnt sacrifices they were offering for the king. He mocked them and swore to burn the Temple down if they did not deliver Judas and his army to him. Overcome with fear, the priests went into the sanctuary and stood before the altar, weeping and imploring the Lord to take revenge on Nicanor and his men because of their blasphemy.

As Judas prepared for battle with Nicanor, he prayed, recalling the occasion when the Lord sent an angel to destroy the army of the Assyrian king, Sennacherib, whose troops outnumbered the troops of the Israelites. That day, an angel killed 185,000 of Sennacherib's troops (see 2 Kings 19:35). Judas implores the Lord to do the same against Nicanor, who blasphemed the Lord's sanctuary.

When the battle began, Nicanor was among the first killed, causing his soldiers to abandon their weapons and flee. The Jews pursued them for a day with other Israelites from all the surrounding villages of Judea coming out to block their retreat and turn them back to face Judas' army. Nicanor's troops were all killed.

After the battle, the Jews collected the spoils, cut off Nicanor's head and his right arm and displayed them in Jerusalem before all the people. The people decreed the day should be observed yearly on the thirteenth day of Adar, March 27, 160 BC. The Jews did not continue to celebrate this feast for long.

## *Lectio Divina*

Spend 8 to 10 minutes in silent contemplation of the following passage:

A dictator of a certain country had such great power he could decide who would be killed or live, who would be thrown into poverty or rewarded with great wealth, or who would be allowed to marry his officers and family members. He contracted cancer and learned he was dying. On his deathbed, he wept and told a confidant, "I don't want to die." It humiliated him to appear weak before the subjects he could once intimidate with a glance. After a life of destruction and killing, Antiochus IV died a lonely, weak man. No one, no matter how powerful, escapes death.

✠ *What can I learn from this passage?*

### Day 4: Death of Judas (8—9:22)

Rome had been steadily growing in power since the end of the third century before Christ. The author of 1 Maccabees details some of the conquests of Rome over the nations and speaks glowingly of the power and organization in Rome. The events portrayed here took place before 63 BC, when the Roman Republic took control of Judea and became a hated ruler over the people. In Judas' era, many nations had great admiration for Rome and entered treaties of peace with the nation.

Judas heard about the valiant fighters of Rome and the Roman custom of establishing friendly relations with the nations siding with Rome. Although the author of Maccabees speaks about Rome's conquest of Gaul, which encompasses a vast area, Gaul in this passage appears to refer to an area of northern Italy and southern France which Rome conquered in 222 BC. Rome enriched itself with Spain's silver and gold mines. In an era of growing strength, the nation crushed and subjected many kings from foreign lands who confronted them. Rome forced Philip and his son, Perseus, the kings of Macedonia, to pay tribute.

According to 1 Maccabees, Rome defeated Antiochus III, the most powerful of the Seleucid kings, who fought against Rome with 120 elephants and a very large army. The actual number of elephants used by Antiochus III was half the number given in 1 Maccabees. Antiochus, who was taken alive, had to agree to pay a heavy tribute, give up a large portion of land, and turn over some hostages. Among the hostages given to Rome was the future Antiochus IV.

Around 146 BC, a Greek force planned to march against Rome. Rome learned about it and sent an army under a single general who took possession of their land, tore down their fortifications, and reduced them to slavery. This revolt occurred after Judas had died. The Roman armies made kings their subjects and made or deposed kings wherever they wished. No one among the Romans became a king. To rule, they established a senate chamber with 320 men to take counsel. They entrust the rule of their government to one man each year. In reality, they usually entrusted the rule to two men.

During the days when many nations either admired or feared the Romans, Judas sent representatives to Rome to establish a friendly alliance. He wanted the help of the Romans against the Greeks. This alliance of peace pleased the Roman senate. In it, the Israelites would fight with Rome or any of its allies if any nation made war on Rome. The nation of Judah promised not to provide supplies to any nation fighting against Rome. When they fight, they shall not seek any compensation. For their part, Rome will in return do exactly as the Israelites promised to do for them. If both parties later agree to add or take away anything from this treaty, they may validly do so.

In the beginning of chapter 9, Demetrius sent Bacchides and Alcimus into the land of Judah along with the right wing of his army. They took the road to Galilee and captured it, killing many people. In 160 BC, when the men in Judas' camp saw the large number of the enemy, they were frightened and began to leave. By the time Judas was to meet Bacchides' force, he had only 800 men. His men tried to talk Judas into going back to their kindred and getting more help, but Judas refused to flee from his opponents. Judas charged the right wing of the army and was winning the battle. When the left wing saw this, they came behind Judas and his army and both sides fought an intense battle. In the midst of the battle, Judas fell and his men fled.

Jonathan and Simon buried their brother, Judas, in the tomb of their ancestors. For many days, Israelites mourned for him, referring to him as the savior of Israel. The author reveals there were other numberless battles that demonstrated the brave deeds and greatness of Judas.

## *Lectio Divina*

Spend 8 to 10 minutes in silent contemplation of the following passage:

> There are men and women like Judas Maccabeus who affected the direction of human history. President Abraham Lincoln freed the slaves, a black woman named Rosa Parks refused to move to the back of a segregated bus, and Nelson Mandela tore down the walls of inequality in South Africa. These are just a few of the heroes whose names people remember and who changed the direction of history for the better. In nations, states, cities, and neighborhoods, there are people who are as important and highly honored as heroes in their own era and area. These are the ones we admire and whose courage and faith we seek to imitate.

✠ *What can I learn from this passage?*

## *Review Questions*

1. How did Mattathias begin the rebellion against Antiochus IV?
2. What were the names of some of the commanders of Antiochus IV's army?
3. What major feast recalls the deeds of Judas Maccabeus, and what were those deeds?
4. How did Judas Maccabeus die?

# The Book of First Maccabees (II)

## 1 MACCABEES 9:23–16

*The land was at rest all the days of Simon, who sought the good of his nation. His rule delighted his people and his glory all his days (14:4).*

**Opening Prayer** (SEE PAGE 15)

## Context

**Part 1: 1 Maccabees (9:23—10:66)** Chapters 9:23 to 10:66 center on Jonathan, who succeeds Judas and becomes high priest. He leads his troops, defeating a man named Apollonius, whom King Demetrius set over a portion of Palestine.

**Part 2: 1 Maccabees (10:67—16)** These chapters consist of a number of treaties between the Jews and Sparta and the Jews and Rome. Jonathan is captured and Simon becomes the leader of the Jews. He becomes a successful and powerful leader of the people.

# PART 1: GROUP STUDY (1 MACCABEES 9:23—10:66)

Read aloud 1 Maccabees 9:23—10:66.

### 9:23-73 Jonathan Succeeds Judas

The Jews who abandoned the Law became known as the lawless ones. With the death of Judas, the lawless Jews spread all kinds of evil throughout the land. According to Jewish law, every seventh year (Sabbath year) the land was left fallow for the sake of the poor and animals (see Exodus 23:10–11). The country made life difficult for the people who were running out of provisions because of the famine. Bacchides, the leader who killed Judas in a previous battle, placed the lawless renegades in charge of the country. The renegades, capturing friends of Judas, brought them to Bacchides, who mocked and punished them. Other friends of Judas asked Judas' brother, Jonathan, to lead them. Unlike Judas, who appointed himself to lead, Jonathan was chosen by the people. He accepted the call.

When Bacchides learned Jonathan was the new leader of the people, he plotted to kill him. Learning about the plot, Jonathan and his brother, Simon, fled into the wilderness to a place near the Dead Sea. Knowing they could not take all their equipment with them, Jonathan chose his brother, John, to lead a convoy to the Nabateans, who helped them in the past. John was to ask the Nabateans to take care of their excess equipment while they fought their battles. During John's journey, however, raiders from Jambri, situated in the northeast of the Dead Sea, captured the convoy and killed John.

A while later, when Jonathan and Simon learned some people of the tribe of Jambri were celebrating a wedding with a large escort bringing the bride to Jambri, Jonathan and Simon sought vengeance for the death of John. They hid their army in the mountains, where a noisy throng with a large amount of baggage would pass. When the bridegroom, along with his friends and kinsmen, came dancing out to meet the bride with tambourines and music, Jonathan's troops rose up and killed or wounded many of them. As the survivors fled to the mountain, Jonathan and his followers plundered their possessions. For the people of Jambri, the joyful songs of the wedding became the sad songs of mourning and lamentations. Having avenged their brother, John's death, Jonathan and Simon returned to the marshes of the Jordan.

When news of the ambush reached Bacchides, he marched with a large force on the Sabbath to the banks of the Jordan, where Jonathan and his men were camped. Jonathan, with the waters of the Jordan behind him and the marshes and thickets on both sides, called out to his men to pray to the heavens and fight for their life. When Bacchides and his forces drew near, Jonathan's troops forced them back. Taking advantage of Bacchides' momentary loss, Jonathan and his companions jumped into the water and swam to the other side. The enemy, having lost 1,000 men in the battle, did not pursue them.

Bacchides returned to Jerusalem and built strongholds in a number of areas in Judea, apparently to defend against Jonathan's guerrilla raids. He placed a garrison in each fortification to send out his own raiding parties to harass the Jews and to protect against Jonathan's guerrilla tactics. For security, Bacchides captured the leading people of the country and kept them as hostages in the fortification (citadel) in Jerusalem.

In May 159 BC, Alcimus, the undeserving high priest, ordered the wall of the inner court of the sanctuary to be torn down. The wall of the inner court separated the holy of holies from the rest of the Temple area. Only the priests could enter the holy of holies. The author states the tearing down of the inner wall amounted to a destruction of the works of the prophets, a reference to Haggai and Zechariah, who helped to supervise the building of the second Temple. As Alcimus began to tear down the inner wall, he was afflicted with a stroke, paralyzing his body and mouth. He died in great agony. The Jews viewed the agonizing death of Alcimus as a punishment from God because Alcimus was changing the Temple structure. When Bacchides learned Alcimus had died, he returned to the king, leaving the land of Judea in peace for two years.

After two years of peace, the lawless Jews felt Jonathan and his companions had grown complacent, making them vulnerable to a surprise attack from Bacchides. They encouraged Bacchides to return to Judah and kill them. When Bacchides set out with a large force, he sent a secret notice to all his allies in Judea, directing them to capture Jonathan and his companions. Jonathan's troops learned of the plot, seized fifty conspiracy leaders, and killed them.

Jonathan and his companions rebuilt the ruins of a fortification in Bethbasi, two miles east of Bethlehem. When Bacchides arrived for battle, he assembled his whole force and constructed siege engines to capture the city. Simon and those with him slipped away from the fortification and, reaching the siege engines, set them on fire. They crushed Bacchides' troops. Enraged with the lawless men who advised him to invade Bacchides killed many of them and returned home. Jonathan sent ambassadors to Bacchides and negotiated a peace treaty with him. As part of the treaty, Bacchides released the Jewish hostages. Although the author reports this release, it never actually took place. Jonathan began to exercise authority over the people.

### 10:1–66 Jonathan Becomes High Priest

In 152 BC, Alexander Epiphanes, who claimed to be the son of Antiochus IV, took over Ptolemais, a prominent Phoenician seacoast city, where he was accepted as king. Since Demetrius had not endeared himself to Rome or to his own subjects, the claim of Alexander as the son of Antiochus was never challenged. When Demetrius heard the people of Ptolemais accepted Alexander as their king, he challenged Alexander in battle. Before he engaged in battle, he wrote a letter to Jonathan seeking peace as an assurance Jonathan would not join Alexander against him.

Demetrius allowed Jonathan to gather an army, and he ordered the release of the Jewish hostages held in the fortress called the citadel. The Gentiles and lawless Jews in the citadel in Jerusalem became frightened when they heard Jonathan could gather an army. They followed the king's orders and released the hostages. Jonathan built a strong wall around Mount Zion, and the followers of Bacchides fled back to their own country.

King Alexander also sent a letter of peace to Jonathan, praising him as a valiant warrior and appointed him high priest. Alexander honored Jonathan, naming him as "the King's Friend" (10:20). Being among the friends of the king was a great honor. The king sent to Jonathan a purple robe and a crown of gold, signs of the high priesthood. Jonathan donned the priestly vestments during the feast of Booths in October 152 BC. He gathered an army and acquired many weapons.

When Demetrius hears Alexander made Jonathan a "Friend," he wrote a letter offering honors and gifts to Jonathan, exempting the Jews from all tribute due on their salt, grain, and fruit. He declared Jerusalem to be sacred and free from all taxes. By giving authority over the Greek fortification of the citadel in Jerusalem to the high priest, Demetrius permitted Jonathan to secure the citadel and guard it as he wished. Although Alexander was the one who appointed Jonathan high priest, Demetrius accepted this appointment in his peace offering. Demetrius proclaimed those in his kingdom who were taken captive from Judea were to be set free. They are to be free from all ransom or taxes due from them or their cattle. He permitted the Jews to celebrate their Sabbaths and feast days, making the three days before the celebrations and three days after a time of exemption for the Jews.

Demetrius allowed the Jews to serve in the king's army with all its privileges and positions of trust and with the right to practice their own Jewish laws. This was a significant honor. He annexed three districts in Samaria to Judea under the single rule of the high priest and allowed the revenue ordinarily sent to Syria to be used for the Temple. Demetrius forgave all personal debts and paid for the restoration of the sanctuary and the walls of Jerusalem.

Jonathan and the people, conscious of the destruction and suffering wrought by Demetrius in Judea, adamantly rejected the gifts offered by Demetrius. In accepting the gifts of Alexander, Jonathan claimed Alexander approached him before Demetrius did. Since Alexander later defeated Demetrius in battle and killed him, the Jews fortunately had chosen the right side.

Alexander, claiming he was now the rightful king of the Seleucids, wrote to Ptolemy, king of Egypt, seeking a peace agreement between the two nations. To solidify the agreement, Alexander married Ptolemy's daughter, Cleopatra, at Ptolemais. Alexander also invited Jonathan to come to Ptolemais, where he met with the two kings and gave them gifts, among them silver and gold. Some of the lawless Jews attempted to accuse Jonathan of evil, but the king ignored them. He clothed Jonathan in royal purple and had him sit at his side. He decreed no one was to make any accusations against Jonathan or trouble him for any reason. When his accusers heard the decree and saw Jonathan clothed in purple, they fled, knowing the king would not favor them. The king enrolled Jonathan among his Chief Friends and made him governor of the province. Jonathan returned in peace and joy to Jerusalem.

## Review Questions

1. What are the differences between the leadership of Judas and Jonathan?
2. What is the significance of making Jonathan high priest?
3. Why were countries so anxious to make treaties with Jonathan?

**Closing Prayer** (SEE PAGE 15)

Pray the closing prayer now or after *lectio divina*.

### *Lectio Divina* (SEE PAGE 8)

Relax your body and maintain a posture of prayer (back straight, eyes shut, feet flat on the floor). This exercise can take as long as you want, but in the context of this Bible study, 10 to 20 minutes should be sufficient.

The meditations that follow are provided only to help group participants use this prayer form, but note that *lectio* is intended to bring one to a place of prayerful contemplation where the Word of God speaks to the hearer from his or her heart. (See page 8 for further instruction.)

### Jonathan Succeeds Judas (9:23–73)

The brothers in the two books of Maccabees show an exceptional trust in God. When they were confronted with impossible situations, they implored the Lord to help them. They offer us an example of trusting God and praying to God in the impossible situations in our life.

✠ *What can I learn from this passage?*

### Jonathan Becomes High Priest (10:1–66)

During the time of the Maccabees, the high priest had a great influence on the life of the people. In the Roman Catholic Church, the pope has a great influence on the Church throughout the world. Just as the Lord provided great leaders with deep faith for the Jewish people during the time of the Maccabees, so the Lord provides spiritual and saintly leaders for the Church throughout history.

✠ *What can I learn from this passage?*

## PART 2: INDIVIDUAL STUDY (1 MACCABEES 10:67—16)

### Day 1: Alliance of Ptolemy and Demetrius II (10:67—11)

In 147 BC, Demetrius II, the son of Demetrius I, rose up against Alexander and appointed Apollonius over Coelesyria, which was originally a region in Lebanon and which later included Palestine. Apollonius encamped at Jamnia, a city in central Israel. He provoked Jonathan into war by reminding him his ancestors were twice forced to flee, an apparent reference to two battles lost by Judas. Jonathan and Simon, with their army, set out from Jerusalem. On their journey, the people of Joppa refused to allow them to enter the city because Apollonius had a garrison there. As they attacked the city, the people became frightened and opened the gates, allowing Jonathan to take control of the city.

Later, when Jonathan's troops pursued Apollonius, he lured the army into a plain where the enemy cavalry could fight more easily. Jonathan pursued Apollonius, who appeared to be fleeing, but Apollonius had hidden 1,000 cavalry behind Jonathan's forces, who rode out of hiding after Jonathan's troops passed by. The army was caught in an ambush, and they fought from morning until night, showered throughout the battle with arrows.

When Apollonius' cavalry had become exhausted, Simon arrived with fresh forces and engaged Apollonius' army in battle, scattering the foot soldiers and cavalry. Jonathan and Simon pursued them into a town named Azotus. They burned and plundered the town and neighboring towns, along with the temple of the idol Dagon and everyone who took refuge in it. Apollonius' army lost about 8,000 warriors in the battle.

Jonathan returned to Jerusalem. When King Alexander heard about the rout of Apollonius, he sent a gold buckle to Jonathan and placed new territories under his control. The gold buckle, which would fasten his cloak at the shoulder, symbolized Jonathan would now be considered one of the King's Kinsmen, the highest court order in the kingdom

In chapter 11, King Ptolemy of Egypt gathered a large army. Feigning peace, he traveled toward Syria. Along the way, the people in the cities, following the orders of Alexander, opened their gates to him. Before he left each city, however, he took control of it by stationing troops there. The people showed the king the burnt temple of Dagon, the charred bodies, and the numerous corpses along the road, but he said nothing. Jonathan met the king at Joppa, and they spent the night in peace. The next day, Jonathan and his army accompanied the king for a short distance and returned to Jerusalem.

King Ptolemy sent ambassadors to King Demetrius, seeking a covenant by offering him his daughter, Cleopatra, the wife of Alexander, whom he intended to conquer. He planned to make Demetrius king of the Seleucid kingdom. Because the people of Crete had revolted against Alexander's kingdom, he was away defending the city. When Alexander heard about the king of Egypt taking possession of his cities, he came back to fight him, but King Ptolemy forced him to flee to Arabia. In Arabia, a man named Zabdiel cut off Alexander's head and sent it to Ptolemy. Three days later, Ptolemy himself was killed and his troops garrisoned in the city strongholds were killed by the inhabitants. Demetrius became king in the summer of 145 BC.

In Jerusalem, Jonathan's forces were storming the citadel. Some of the lawless Jews went to King Demetrius and informed him about the siege. In a fit of anger, Demetrius wrote to Jonathan to cease the siege and meet him at Ptolemais. Jonathan did not lift the siege, but he went to the king with silver, gold, and garments. Surprisingly, the king liked Jonathan and treated him well, just as his predecessors had done. He affirmed Jonathan as high priest and in the positions of honor he previously held. He also enrolled him among his Chief Friends.

At Jonathan's request, the king exempted Judea and the three districts in Samaria from paying tribute. The king sent Jonathan and the Jewish nation a copy of a letter he sent to a trusted friend, Lasthenes, concerning the benefits granted the Jewish nation for their goodwill toward them. The letter spoke of the exemptions given to Judea and the districts of Samaria, freeing them from paying tribute and from all other obligations previously promised by Demetrius I.

When King Demetrius saw the land was peaceful, he dismissed his army except for the foreign mercenaries. He apparently did not pay his dismissed troops as his predecessors did. By paying them, they would loyally return for battle when needed. Lacking this pay, the soldiers became hostile to Demetrius.

When a man named Trypho, once faithful to Alexander, heard the grumbling of the soldiers, he plotted to take over the kingship. He persuaded an Arabian guardian of Alexander's son, Antiochus, to give him the son to succeed his father.

Jonathan sent word to Demetrius to remove his troops from the citadel in Jerusalem and from other strongholds. Demetrius stalled, telling Jonathan he would do it as soon as he had the opportunity. In the meantime, since many of his own troops abandoned him, he needed help from the Jews. Jonathan sent 3,000 troops to him.

The people rebelled and gained control of the main streets in preparation for a battle against Demetrius. The Jewish force came to his aid, spreading throughout the city and killing about 100,000 people and setting the city on fire. When the people saw the massacre by the Jews, they begged the king to accept peace and stop the Jews from attacking them and the city. The people surrendered their weapons and made peace. The king honored the Jews and gave them a large amount of plunder to take back to Jerusalem. Unfortunately, the king soon changed his attitude toward Jonathan and afflicted him with great anguish.

When Trypho returned with Antiochus and made him king, the soldiers—embittered because Demetrius refused to pay them—rallied around the new king and routed Demetrius, who had to flee. The young Antiochus confirmed Jonathan's high priesthood, appointed him ruler over four districts, and made him one of the king's Friends. He sent Jonathan gold dishes, gave him the right to drink from gold cups, to dress in royal purple, and to wear a gold buckle. He made Simon governor of the coastal area of Egypt.

When Jonathan passed through the area of Palestine and Coelesyria, he was well-received everywhere except for Gaza. When the people of Gaza tried to shut him out, he burned and plundered Gaza's suburbs, leading the people of Gaza to plead for peace. Jonathan sent the sons of their leaders to Jerusalem as hostages who could be killed if the people rebelled against Jonathan. When Jonathan learned Demetrius sent a powerful force against him in Galilee, he left his brother, Simon, to attack Beth-zur, an enemy stronghold, and went to meet Demetrius' generals in battle. Simon captured Beth-zur.

The next day, Jonathan attacked the forces of Demetrius' generals. Unfortunately, he again marched his army into an ambush. The enemy mounted a frontal attack and, in the midst of the battle, those hiding rose and attacked Jonathan's forces from behind. All of Jonathan's troops fled, except the army commanders, Mattathias and Judas. Jonathan tore his garments, threw dust on his head, and prayed. He then joined the battle with the commanders and routed the enemy. When Jonathan's fleeing warriors saw this, they turned back to the battle. About 3,000 foreign troops were killed in the battle. Jonathan then returned to Jerusalem.

### Lectio Divina

Spend 8 to 10 minutes in silent contemplation of the following passage:

When Jesus sent his disciples on a mission, he told them, "Behold, I am sending you like sheep in the midst of wolves; so be shrewd as serpents and simple as doves" (Matthew 10:16). Jonathan often sought peace, but he had to be as wise as a serpent in dealing with deceitful leaders. He was protecting the Temple and the people in the midst of wolves. Loving and trusting people in a world where many are seeking their own good at the expense of others demands great wisdom.

✠ *What can I learn from this passage?*

## Day 2: Capture of Jonathan (12)

To relieve some of the pressure from wars with foreign powers, Jonathan decided to renew the friendship Judea had with Rome and Sparta. Although Sparta was a declining power in Greece, it could still mount an army for war.

In Jonathan's letter to Rome, he declares that he as the high priest and the Jewish people seek to renew their friendship and alliance with Rome. The Romans received the message in friendship and gave to Jonathan's envoys letters addressed to authorities in various places to provide the envoys with safe passage back to the land of Judah.

In Jonathan's letter to the Spartans, he declares that he as the high priest, the senate of the nation, the priests, and the rest of the Jewish people send greetings to their brothers, the Spartans. He sends with his envoys a copy of a letter written long before by King Arius I (309–265 BC) to Onias, who was high priest from 323 to 300 BC. In the letter, he states the Jews and Spartans are brothers. When the Spartan envoy came to the Israelites, Onias welcomed them with honor. Jonathan's letter sought an alliance in a spirit of friendship.

Jonathan writes the Jews have no need of such a letter and such an alliance, since they possess the holy books for their encouragement. The holy books appear to refer to the Scriptures. Despite the protection offered by the holy books, Jonathan declares the Jews seek to renew their friendship with the Spartans so they do not become strangers. Jonathan states the Jews remembered them in their sacrifices and prayers, as is proper for brothers to do.

Jonathan notes the Jews did not trouble the Spartans when kings of the surrounding nations attacked them. They had heaven (God) as their protector, who saved them by defeating their enemies. Now, Jonathan is sending two envoys to them and to Rome to renew their friendship and alliance. He requests a reply.

The author refers to the letter from Arius to Onias. Greeting Onias as high priest, Arius claims the Spartans found a document stating the Spartans and Jews are brothers belonging to the family of Abraham. The custom of claiming a common lineage was occasionally used in ancient time in seeking peace. Arius asks the Israelites to inform him about their welfare and states the animals and possessions of both nations are shared in common.

Jonathan received word the officers of Demetrius gathered together a stronger army than before to attack Jonathan's troops. To keep Demetrius' forces from entering his province, Jonathan left Jerusalem and traveled north to a placed named Hamath, which was at the northeastern end of his territory. When the two armies were encamped within the same vicinity, Jonathan, who apparently had the larger force, heard from his spies the enemy was preparing a surprise attack that night. Jonathan ordered his men to be alert, and when Demetrius' soldiers realized Jonathan knew of their plan, they became afraid and remained in their camp. In the morning, Jonathan went to attack them, but they had abandoned the camp. Jonathan then turned in a different direction and successfully engaged some Arabians in a battle.

In the meanwhile, Simon, who heard the people of Joppa were going to turn their city over to the supporters of Demetrius, captured Joppa and left a garrison there to guard it. Jonathan returned to Jerusalem to build up its fortifications with a higher wall between the citadel and the city. The citadel remained in the hands of the enemy.

Although Trypho had designs on becoming king of Asia by killing King Antiochus V, he feared Jonathan would not permit this to happen and would kill him. One day, when Jonathan went to meet Trypho with 40,000 troops, Trypho became frightened and decided to greet Jonathan with honor, introduce him to his friends, and offer him gifts. He ordered his friends and soldiers to obey Jonathan as they would him. Feigning peace, he enticed Jonathan to send home most of his troops and keep only a small number with him. He persuaded Jonathan to come with him to Ptolemais so he could hand the stronghold over to Jonathan with other strongholds. Jonathan trusted him and kept only 3,000 troops with him, dismissing the rest. He left 2,000 in Galilee and took 1,000 with him to Ptolemais.

When Jonathan and those with him entered the city, the people closed the gates behind them. They seized and killed his army and arrested Jonathan. Trypho sent soldiers and cavalry to Galilee to destroy the 2,000 men left behind, but they were prepared to fight. When their enemy saw this, they turned back to their stronghold.

Believing Jonathan was killed along with the troops accompanying him, Jonathan's army returned safely to the land of Judah and mourned Jonathan's death and the death of those who were with him. As news of Jonathan's death spread, the nations around Judah supposed the Jews were left without a leader, so they decided to totally erase the memory of Judah from the earth.

### Lectio Divina

Spend 8 to 10 minutes in silent contemplation of the following passage:

Although Jonathan was a valiant warrior, there were signs he did not cherish war. He sought peace where he could find it, and he trusted others too easily. The Scriptures reveal those who seek their own power and deceive others in order to gain from them often end up suffering a violent death themselves. The good may suffer, but they find more meaning and faith in their suffering. They teach the foolishness of seeking power or prestige by evil means.

✠ *What can I learn from this passage?*

## Day 3: Leadership of Simon (13)

Simon learned Trypho was gathering a large army to attack Judea. When he saw how frightened the Jews were, he went to Jerusalem and, assembling the people, reminded them about the exploits of his brothers and father. Like his brothers who perished for the nation, he was willing to die as they did. Asserting the Gentiles have united to destroy them, he vowed to avenge Judah and the sanctuary, along with the wives and children of the men of the nation. When the people heard Simon's words, they accepted him as their leader. Gathering all the able-bodied men and hastening to finish building the walls of Jerusalem, Simon sent warriors, under the command of a man named Jonathan, to Joppa to drive out the inhabitants and remain in the city to protect it against Trypho.

When Trypho learned the people had chosen Simon as their leader and intended to fight him, he sent envoys to Simon, saying he was holding Jonathan hostage because of the money Jonathan owed the royal treasury in connection with the offices he held. He told Simon to send silver and Jonathan's two sons as hostages to guarantee Jonathan will not rebel against him (Trypho). Simon faced a dilemma. He knew Trypho was deceiving him and would most likely kill Jonathan no matter what he did, but he feared provoking hostility among his people if he did not agree to Trypho's commands. He did as Trypho demanded, and, as he expected, Trypho did not release Jonathan.

Trypho attempted to attack Jerusalem, but Simon blocked him in every attempt. The enemy in the citadel, desperate for provisions, sent envoys to Trypho to come to them through the wilderness, but a heavy snowstorm hindered him, so he left for Gilead. On the journey home, he had Jonathan killed and buried. Simon sent for the remains of Jonathan and buried him in Modein, the city of his ancestors, where the people mourned over him and built a magnificent monument of tall polished stones and seven pyramids facing one another, representing his father and mother, his four brothers, and apparently one for himself (Simon).

Trypho killed young King Antiochus and became king. Simon made his strongholds even more secure and sent some men to King Demetrius to obtain an exemption from the taxes. King Demetrius received the gifts of peace Simon sent and agreed to a lasting peace, granting him exemption from the taxes and giving him the right to keep his strongholds. As a result, in the year 141 BC, the people began to date their records and contracts with the opening citation: "In the first year of Simon, great high priest, governor, and leader of the Jews" (13:42).

Simon led an attack against Gazara, a major fortification of the Greeks. His men made a siege machine, captured one of the towers, and forced their way into the fortification. The people in the city climbed the wall with their garments rent and cried to Simon to grant them terms of peace. Simon agreed. He expelled them from the city and purified the houses of their pagan idols. After entering the city with songs of praise, he settled the people who observed the Law there. He fortified the stronghold and built himself a residence.

The enemy, trapped in the citadel in Jerusalem and dying of starvation, petitioned for terms of peace. Simon agreed to a peace settlement and expelled them from the citadel. After cleansing the citadel of its impurities, the Jews entered the citadel with shouts of praise, waving palm branches, playing on harps, cymbals, and lyres, and singing hymns of praise. Since the time of Antiochus IV, the citadel was at the center of conflicts in Jerusalem.

Because the conquest of the citadel was so important, Simon decreed the day should be celebrated with joy every year. Simon and his people dwelt in the citadel and strengthened the fortifications of the Temple mount alongside the citadel. Since his son, John Hyrcanus (134–104 BC), was now old enough to lead soldiers, Simon appointed him commander of the soldiers at Gazara.

## Lectio Divina

Spend 8 to 10 minutes in silent contemplation of the following passage:

Jonathan and his brothers laid down their life for the Temple and the people. Accepting martyrdom for a worthy cause is difficult, but it proves the depth of one's love. Jesus said, "No one has greater love than this, to lay down one's life for one's friends" (John 15:13). Jesus laid down his life for everyone, proving God's great love for everyone. Jonathan and his brothers expressed their great love for God and the people of their nation in fighting for the nation.

✠ *What can I learn from this passage?*

## Day 4: Praise of Simon (14)

In 140 BC, King Demetrius II marched into Media, where a general of the king of Persia and Media captured him and brought him to their king, Arsaces.

The author inserts a song of praise in honor of Simon, listing his successes. It speaks about the land being at rest during his time as the leader of the people. The peace refers to the lack of war between the people of Judea and the Seleucid kings. His rule brought delight to his people and glory to him, especially his conquest of Joppa, which opened the roads to the nations to the sea. He gained a larger expanse of land for the nation and took many prisoners, making himself master of strongholds such as Gazara, Beth-zur, and the citadel. Because he captured the citadel in Jerusalem, the people could cultivate their land in peace, which could now bear abundant fruit. The peace allowed the old men to sit in the squares as they did in the past, reminiscing about the good times, while the young men donned armor.

Simon, who supplied food and provided a strong defense for the people, became known to the ends of the earth. The people enjoyed peace, relaxing undisturbed under their vines and fig trees. Simon crushed kings and aggressors, strengthened those zealous for the law, and destroyed the lawless and wicked. He brought splendor to the sanctuary and increased its furnishings.

At the news of Jonathan's death, the people of Rome and Sparta grieved, and when they learned Simon, his brother, was the new high priest, they sent him inscribed tablets of bronze to renew the alliance and friendship they established with his brothers, Judas and Jonathan. The Spartans declared the letter of peace received by the Jews was recorded in the public archives so the people of Sparta would have a record of them. These letters of peace would be helpful to the people and future generations. Simon then sent his ambassador to Rome with a large gold shield to confirm the alliance with Rome.

By forging inscriptions of honor on bronze tablets and attaching them to the pillars on Mount Zion, the people of Judea demonstrated their gratitude to Simon, his brother, and his father's household for bringing them freedom. They dated their proclamation as taking place on September 13, 140 BC, and as the third year under Simon. Because Mattathias' family resisted the enemies of the nation and preserved the Law and sanctuary from destruction and abomination, the people of Judea praised the brothers for willingly placing themselves in danger and bringing glory to the nation.

The inscription on the bronze tablets speaks first of Jonathan, who rallied the nation, became the high priest, and was killed. It next told of the exploits of Simon, who fought for the nation and spent his own money to equip his forces and pay them. Ordinarily the treasury would provide funds, but it appears to have been depleted or plundered. Simon settled his forces in the cities of Judea, especially the border city of Beth-zur. He also fortified Joppa and Gazara, restoring them and settling Jews in them. When the people realized the fidelity of Simon and the glory he brought to their land, they chose him as their leader and high priest. He succeeded in driving the Gentiles out of Jerusalem and out of the citadel in Jerusalem. By stationing his soldiers in the citadel and fortifying its walls, he made it a stronghold for the protection of Jerusalem and the countryside.

When King Demetrius heard the Romans acclaimed the Jews to be friends, allies, and brothers, he showered great honors on Simon in an effort to keep him from siding with the Romans if that nation should fight against him. He heard the Romans received Simon's envoys to their city with great honor. He also heard the Jewish people and priests asked Simon to be their high priest until a prophet appeared. For a long time, no prophet arose among the people. If one should happen to appear, then he would decide whether Simon's descendants should continue as high priest. The letter declares Simon shall be the leader of the people in their internal affairs, in their battles, and in their relations with other nations. As high priest, he shall protect the sanctuary and wear the purple garments and a gold buckle. All the Jews must obey him.

Simon accepted the role of high priest and leadership given to him by the people and priests. A decree declared the appointment of Simon to these offices is to be engraved on a bronze tablet hung in a conspicuous place in the sanctuary and copies of it deposited in the treasury where they would be available for Simon and his sons.

## *Lectio Divina*

Spend 8 to 10 minutes in silent contemplation of the following passage:

Simon can be proud to bear the name of such a courageous family. People who are baptized bear the name Christian. Just as Simon lived up to the name of his family, we pray all the baptized will live up to the name of their spiritual family—Christian. Christians are called to courageously remain faithful to the family of Jesus, just as the Maccabees did.

✠ *What can I learn from this passage?*

---

### Day 5: Antiochus VII (15—16)

Antiochus VII, the son of Demetrius, sent a letter to Simon, the priests, and the Jewish nation, stating his intentions to reclaim—with the help of a large number of mercenary troops and warships—the land seized from his kingdom. Renewing the terms of peace Simon made with King Demetrius, Antiochus granted Jerusalem the right to coin its own money and keep possession of all its weapons. He canceled all debts owed to the royal treasury and promised to honor the nation and Temple once he reclaimed his kingdom.

In 138 BC, Antiochus VII invaded the land of his ancestors and forced Trypho to flee to Dor by the sea, a fortress on the coast of Palestine. Antiochus surrounded the city with his troops on the land and his ships nearby at sea.

In the meanwhile, Rome sent a letter to many kings and nations, informing them Simon and the Jewish people sent ambassadors to Rome to renew their friendship. They offered him a golden shield as a sign of their friendship. Rome decided to accept the shield and ordered the countries to turn over to Simon any troublemakers from his country who seek asylum with them. The letter also warned the nations neither to fight against them nor to support those who battle with them.

Antiochus assaulted Dor. Simon sent 2,000 troops along with silver, gold, and equipment to Antiochus to help in the siege, but Antiochus rejected them and broke all the agreements made with Simon, whom he now considered an enemy. He sent a Friend to Simon, informing him the Jews are occupying Joppa and Gazara and the citadel of Jerusalem, which he claimed are districts of his kingdom. He ordered Simon to give up the cities and the tribute received from these districts or pay him 500 talents of silver for the devastation they caused and another 500 for the tribute money of the cities Simon controlled outside of Judea. He warned Simon his army will come and attack him if he does not meet his demands.

Simon responded his army had not taken foreign land or the property of others, but only the heritage of their ancestors which was held unjustly by their enemies. Because these cities were harming the Jewish people and their country, his army occupied Joppa and Gazara. Simon offered 100 talents to the envoy for these cities, but he gave no answer before returning to Antiochus. When he told the king about Simon's response, the splendor of Simon's court, the gold and silver plates, and his wealth, the king flew into a rage.

At Dor, Trypho boarded a ship and escaped from Antiochus' trap. Antiochus appointed a man named Cendebeus and ordered him to fortify Kedron, which was just opposite the fortress of Gazara held by John Hyrcanus. He wanted him to wage war on the people of Judea. After Cendebeus entered the fortification, his army launched raids into Judea, capturing people and slaughtering them. Following the commands of Antiochus, he stationed infantry and cavalry at Kedron so they could patrol the roads to Judea.

In chapter 16, Simon's son, John, left Gazara and reported to Simon what Cendebeus was doing. Summoning Judas and John, Simon's two oldest sons, Simon recalled how he, his brothers, and his father successfully fought for Israel since their youth. Since he is now old, he sends his sons to fight for the nation and prays the help of heaven (God) will be with them.

John gathered a force of 20,000 warriors and cavalry and went to battle against Cendebeus. In the plain where the battle was to take place, a wadi lay between the two armies. When John realized his army was afraid to cross the wadi and face the large army of Cendebeus, he attacked first and his army followed him into battle. Many of the enemy were killed and fell wounded, while the rest fled toward their stronghold. In the battle, Judas was wounded and John pursued Cendebeus' army to Kedron. When some of the enemy took refuge in the towers as they fled, John set the towers on fire, killing about 2,000 troops. He then returned to Judea.

Ptolemy, the son-in-law of Simon, was appointed governor of the plain of Jericho and had amassed a large amount of silver and gold. He plotted to kill Simon and his sons so he could gain control of the country. In 134 BC, Simon and his sons, Mattathias and Judas, went to Jericho, where Ptolemy deceitfully welcomed them in a stronghold he built. After hiding his men in the banquet hall, he served Simon and his sons a sumptuous banquet. When Simon and his sons were drunk, Ptolemy and his men killed them and some of their servants.

Ptolemy sent a letter to King Antiochus, asking the king to turn over to him the towns and country. He sent men to Gazara to kill John. He then sent letters to John's army officers, inviting them to come to him so he could give them silver, gold, and other gifts. He sent others to seize Jerusalem and the Temple mount. Before he went to Gazara to kill John, someone ran ahead to alert John about the death of his father and brothers and warn him Ptolemy is sending men to kill him. When the men arrived, John captured and killed them.

The remainder of the deeds of John, including his wars and brave acts, his rebuilding of the walls, and all his achievements are recorded in the chronicles of the high priesthood, from the time he succeeded his father as high priest.

### Lectio Divina

Spend 8 to 10 minutes in silent contemplation of the following passage:

In the Old Testament, the Lord refers to the Israelites as the special people of God. As we read the history of the nation, it appears to be a miraculous history of survival. Many times the nation could have been decimated and wiped off the face of the earth, but they survived and prospered. Their survival alone illustrates God's protection and love of the Chosen People.

✠ *What can I learn from this passage?*

## Review Questions

1. Why did Demetrius and Alexander try to lure Jonathan to back them?
2. Who is Trypho and what did he accomplish?
3. What are some accomplishments of Simon?

# The Book of Second Maccabees

## 2 MACCABEES 1–15

*In doing this he acted in a very excellent and noble way, inasmuch as he had the resurrection in mind; for if he were not expecting the fallen to rise again, it would have been superfluous and foolish to pray for the dead (12:43–44).*

**Opening Prayer** (SEE PAGE 15)

## Context

**Part 1: 2 Maccabees (1—2)** The Book of 2 Maccabees is not a continuation of the history of the Maccabees found in 1 Maccabees. A theological reflection on the period dominated by Judas Maccabeus is found in 2 Maccabees. The central theological themes concern the Temple and God's intervention in the history of the Jews.

The opening chapters present two letters sent from the Jews in Jerusalem to the Jews in Egypt, urging them to celebrate the feast of Hanukkah. The author declares he is summarizing a history (which no longer exists) by a writer named Jason in North Africa.

**Part 2: 2 Maccabees (3—15)** The Book of 2 Maccabees speaks more of God's direct intervention in the battles of Judas than does 1 Maccabees. The integrity of the Temple and the explanation of the feast of Hanukkah become central. The book speaks of life after death and the noble practice of making atonement for the dead.

## PART 1: GROUP STUDY (2 MACCABEES 1—2)

Read aloud 2 Maccabees 1—2.

### *1—2:18 Letters to Jews in Egypt*

The Jews, residing in Jerusalem and the land of Jude, send the first of two letters to the large Jewish community living in Egypt. The first letter, apparently written in 124 BC, begins with the usual Greek practice of greeting the reader. The author prays God will treat the recipients well, as was the case with their ancestors, Abraham, Isaac, and Jacob. The Jews in Jerusalem pray the community in Egypt will have the heart to worship and follow God's will and commands. They hope God will hear their prayers and not abandon them in times of adversity.

In the year 143 BC, during the reign of Demetrius, king of Syria, the Jews in Judea penned a previous letter referred to by the writer of this letter. The letter concerned the distress caused by Jason and his followers, who revolted against the Holy Land and kingdom. Jason, the high priest, introduced many Greek customs and constructions in the Holy Land. He set fire to the gate house and slaughtered a number of people (see 2 Maccabees 4:7–22). The people in Judea prayed for help from God, offering sacrifices and worshiping God in accord with their laws. The Lord answered their prayers in the successful battles of the Maccabees. In memory of this event, the author reminds the people to celebrate the feast of Booths (Hanukkah) on the twenty-fifth of Kislev (November or December).

The second letter comes from the people of Jerusalem and Judea along with members of the senate and Judas, their leader. They send good wishes to the Jews in Egypt and to Aristobulus, whom the letter claims was a teacher of King Ptolemy and a member of the anointed priestly family. The people thank God for saving them from the grave perils which were brought upon them by Antiochus IV, whose stronger force was savagely beaten by the Persians.

According to a story heard by the author of the letter, Antiochus came to the temple of a Syrian goddess, Nanea, to marry her, an action performed by a representative. He actually hoped to gain wealth from that temple. When Antiochus and a few attendants went into the temple precincts, the priests locked them inside, opened a secret trap door in the ceiling and killed the king and his attendants by hurling rocks at them. They dismembered their bodies, cut off their heads, and threw them to the people. This is one of several stories concerning the death of Antiochus.

The author gives reasons for celebrating Hanukkah, making use of a legendary story of a fire from the altar of the first Temple that was hidden in the hollow of a cistern when the Israelites went into Persian exile. Actually, the Israelites went into exile in Babylon. In the story, the priests went to find the fire after the exile, but in its place they found a thick liquid. Nehemiah directed the priests to sprinkle the liquid on the wood and on the material for the sacrifices on the altar. When the sun began to shine, a fire burst out on the altar, amazing the crowd. As the sacrifice burned, the priests and the assembly prayed.

The people pray God will free and gather together the Jews living as slaves among Gentiles, thus showing them the power of the God of Israel. After the sacrifice was consumed, the priests sang hymns of praise. Nehemiah directed the priests to pour the rest of the liquid on large slabs. When they poured the liquid on the stone, a fire blazed up, but the light of the fire was overwhelmed by the light on the altar. When the king learned where the priests had hidden the fire and found in its place a thick liquid, he had a fence built around the place.

Chapter 2 refers to a record declaring Jeremiah the prophet ordered the deportees to take some of the fire with them and told them not to forget the laws of the Lord and not be led astray when they see the gold and silver gods and their adornments. According to the letter, the same document states Jeremiah gave the order for the tent and ark to accompany him into exile. In reality, Jeremiah did not go into Babylonian exile in 597 BC. Jeremiah told the people the place is to remain unknown. When the time comes for revealing it, the glory of the Lord and the cloud will be seen as it was in the time of Moses and Solomon (Exodus 40:34–35; 1 Kings 8:11).

The letter states how fire consumed the offerings made by Solomon as it did for Moses (see 2 Chronicles 7:1 and Leviticus 9:23–24). Solomon celebrated for eight days. The letter speaks of a library founded by Nehemiah, but there is no record of Nehemiah founding a library. Just as the people of Jerusalem were about to celebrate Hanukkah, so the Jews in Egypt should do the same, celebrating it as the time when God saved his people, the kingdom, the priesthood, and the sacred rites.

### 2:19–32 Compiler's Preface

The compiler states this is the story of Judas Maccabeus and his brothers. The celebration of Hanukkah had its origin in the independence won by the Maccabees who fought against Antiochus IV Epiphanes and Antiochus V Eupator. It is a story of the purification of the Temple and the dedication of the altar. They regained possession of the Temple, liberated Jerusalem, and reestablished the laws that were in danger of being abolished. The compiler refers to the five-volume work of Jason of Cyrene which no longer exists.

The author of 2 Maccabees claims he undertook the difficult task of making a digest of the records of the events he is about to report. Making a comparison between an architect who plans the whole structure and the decorator who is concerned only with the adornments, the author declares he will leave the details to the historian and aim to keep his adaptation brief and not as detailed.

## Review Questions

1. What is the feast of Hanukkah?
2. What is the story of the sacred fire?
3. What does the author of 2 Maccabees say about his story?

_____

**Closing Prayer** (SEE PAGE 15)

Pray the closing prayer now or after *lectio divina*.

_____

**Lectio Divina** (SEE PAGE 8)

Relax your body and maintain a posture of prayer (back straight, eyes shut, feet flat on the floor). This exercise can take as long as you want, but in the context of this Bible study, 10 to 20 minutes should be sufficient.

The meditations that follow are provided only to help group participants use this prayer form, but note that *lectio* is intended to bring one to a place of prayerful contemplation where the Word of God speaks to the hearer from his or her heart. (See page 8 for further instruction.)

_____

### Letters to Jews in Egypt (1—2:18)

The celebration of major Jewish feasts in different nations brought the Jewish community together in prayer. Christian churches also celebrate common feasts, such as Easter, on the same day in a variety of nations. In doing this, they are not only celebrating the feast day but also celebrating the unity in prayer of a community in love with God.

✠ *What can I learn from this passage?*

### Compiler's Preface (2:19–32)

Although religions honor God and recognize the power of God in creation, they also realize God has given the world certain heroes as examples and saviors of the faith throughout history. The Maccabees are the saints who offered their lives to preserve faith in God and loyalty to the covenant. The Old and New Testament tell of saints who gave their lives for love of God. They still exist in the world today, and they need our prayers.

✠ *What can I learn from this passage?*

## PART 2: INDIVIDUAL STUDY (2 MACCABEES 3—15)

## Day 1: Influence of High Priests in Judea (3—5)

The author introduces an idealized story meant to enhance the glory of the Temple in Jerusalem and God's delight with the people who honored the Law and the Temple. Due to the piety of Onias III, the high priest (196–175 BC), the king showered special gifts on the Temple. Seleucus IV, king of Asia (187—175 BC), did not tax the expenses necessary for the liturgy of sacrifice. In Jerusalem, a man named Simon, who belonged to the priestly family of Bilgah (see 1 Chronicles 24:14), was a superintendent of the Temple. Disagreeing with Onias about the administration of the city market, he reported to an official named Apollonius about a large sum of assets not belonging to the account of the sacrifices and therefore not exempt from taxation.

When Apollonius informed the king about the untaxed assets, the king sent his chief minister, Heliodorus, to Jerusalem to seize the possessions from

Onias. Onias received Heliodorus graciously and explained to him the funds were for the sake of the orphans and widows and some belonged to Hyrcanus, a man who held a very high position in Jerusalem. Besides, explained Onias, the sum was not as large as reported but consisted of only 400 talents of silver and 200 of gold. Onias added he would not defraud those who trusted in the holiness of the place and the sacredness of a Temple esteemed all over the world.

When Heliodorus followed the king's orders and seized the assets, the entire populace suffered anguish. The deplorable appearance of the high priest revealed his mental torment. The priests in their priestly robes pleaded with the Lord to keep the assets safe. The people crowded together in anguish, with the women wearing sackcloth and the young women, ordinarily kept in seclusion, rushing out and crying with their hands raised heavenward. The people lay prostrate throughout the city, begging the Lord to protect the deposits.

When Heliodorus and his bodyguards arrived at the treasury, they encountered a vision so terrifying the guards fainted. A horse and a terrifying rider appeared and charged toward Heliodorus. The horse attacked Heliodorus with its front hoofs. Two handsome and powerful men appeared on each side of Heliodorus and flogged him unceasingly until he fell to the ground, where a great darkness engulfed him. Astounded at the awesome power of God, Heliodorus' men carried his helpless body away.

When the people saw what happened, their anguish turned to rejoicing. Heliodorus' men begged Onias to pray to the Most High to save their leader, who was near death. Onias, fearing the king would punish the Jews for the beating of Heliodorus, offered a sacrifice for him. While he was offering his sacrifice, Heliodorus saw the same two men who flogged him appear to inform him the Lord has spared his life because of Onias' sacrifice. They instruct Heliodorus, who was scourged by heaven (God), to proclaim God's supreme power. Having said this, they disappeared.

After Heliodorus offered a sacrifice to the Lord, he bade farewell to Onias and returned to the king, bearing witness to the accomplishments of God. When the king asked who he should send to Jerusalem next, Heliodorus told him he should send an enemy and receive him back with a flogging if he survives. He declared the one dwelling in heaven watches over the place and punishes those who attempt to harm it.

In chapter 4, Simon continued to slander Onias and incited Apollonius to join in his wickedness. Realizing the king may believe Simon and Apollonius, Onias appealed to the king, not to accuse his opponents but as one seeking the safety of all the people. He believed Simon would not cease his evil actions, and his people could not live in peace unless he himself had the attention of the king.

Before Onias could complete his mission, King Seleucus died and his brother, who became Antiochus IV, eventually ascended to the throne. The king ordinarily chose as high priest someone who paid the largest amount, not as a bribe but as an expected payment. Jason, Onias' brother, promised to pay a large sum to the king for the office of high priest and another large sum if the king gave him the authority to build a gymnasium and a youth center. Jason admired the Greek culture to the degree he wanted to enroll the citizens of Jerusalem as citizens of the Greek city of Antioch. He abandoned the practice of Jewish law and introduced customs contrary to them.

He had a gymnasium built at the foot of the citadel and persuaded the young men to wear the Greek hat. The citadel in Jerusalem was a stronghold held by the king's army. Even the priests favored the introduction of the Greek culture and no longer had an interest in the services at the altar. They enjoyed the Greek games and exercises contrary to the Law in the gymnasium.

During a celebration of Greek games, Jason sent to Hercules a large sum of money for the sacrifice, but those entrusted with the money decided it was a waste to spend it on the sacrifice, so they used it to buy war vessels. Later, when Apollonius learned the king was not in favor of his policies, he fled to Phoenicia, going through Jerusalem, where Jason and the people received him with great splendor.

Three years later, Jason sent a man named Menelaus to negotiate with the king on some urgent matters, and Menelaus, while with the king, outbid the amount Jason promised to pay for his office and returned as the new high priest. Menelaus served cruelly as high priest and never paid the king as he promised. The king summoned him and the commandant of the citadel, who was appointed to the fruitless task of collecting the sum from Menelaus. Menelaus left his brother, Lysimachus, and his deputy in charge while he was away.

The king had to attend to a revolt within the kingdom, so he left as his deputy a noble named Andronicus. Menelaus stole some gold vessels from the Temple and gave them to Andronicus. When Onias had evidence of the Menelaus' thefts from the Temple, he accused Menelaus publicly, after Onias withdrew to a safe sanctuary near Antioch. Menelaus convinced Andronicus to feign friendship with Onias to lure him out of the sanctuary and to kill him, which he did.

The Jews and people of other nations became angry over the unjust murder of Onias. When the king returned and learned of Andronicus' act, he became furious and ordered his men to strip off the purple cloak symbolizing Andronicus' high position and the rest of his garments and lead him through the town to the very spot where he murdered Onias. The author views this execution as being delivered by the will of the Lord.

Lysimachus, with the help of Menelaus, stole a large number of gold vessels from the Temple. When the people rioted, Lysimachus initiated an attack against them with 3,000 armed men. In defense, the people hurled stones, pieces of wood, and ashes at Lysimachus and his troops. They wounded a number of them and killed a few. The rest fled. Lysimachus, referred to by the author as the "temple robber (4:42)," was killed near the treasury.

Because Menelaus connived with Lysimachus to steal the gold vessels, he had to appear before the king to defend himself. When Menelaus realized the trial was going against him, he promised Ptolemy a substantial sum of money to change the king's mind. Ptolemy persuaded the king, and Menelaus was acquitted while those who would have been declared innocent even if they appeared before the ruthless Scythians were unjustly punished. Menelaus remained in office, becoming more wicked and continually scheming against his own people.

In chapter 5, when Antiochus IV began a second invasion of Egypt, the people in Jerusalem saw a vision for forty days of a battle of fully armed troops and cavalry. The people prayed the vision was a good omen.

When Jason heard a rumor about the death of Antiochus, he gathered at least 1,000 troops and captured Jerusalem. Jason slaughtered many of the people of the city. Instead of gaining control of the government, however, he only brought shame to himself. He had to flee from city to city, hated as an apostate and loathed for slaughtering his own people. He died in exile without a funeral and without a place in the tomb of his ancestors.

When the king heard of the battle in Judea, he thought Judea was in revolt and he left Egypt. He slaughtered the people in Judea, ordering his soldiers to slay anyone they encountered in the streets or in their homes. They slaughtered the young and old, women and children, young mothers with their infants, killing 40,000 inhabitants and selling 40,000 into slavery.

Antiochus entered the sacred Temple with Menelaus as his guide. With his impure hands, he gathered the sacred vessels and votive offerings given by previous kings for the honor and glory of the Temple. Antiochus became proud of his accomplishments, unaware his conquests were the result of the anger of the Lord against the sins of the people. If the people had not sinned, the Lord would have punished Antiochus the same way the Lord punished Heliodorus. The Temple shared in the fate of the people, being blessed when the people remained faithful to the Law and profaned when the people were unfaithful.

Antiochus left the governors to harass and treat the nation of Judea with great cruelty. He left as high priest Menelaus, who ruled the people worse than in the past. He sent Apollonius to head an army of 22,000 with orders to murder all the men and sell the women and children into slavery. Apollonius at first pretended to come in peace to Jerusalem, and on a Sabbath day—when the Jews were abstaining from work—he marched through Jerusalem with his army, killing a large number of people. Judas Maccabeus and about nine others fled to the wilderness and lived like animals in the hills.

### Lectio Divina

Spend 8 to 10 minutes in silent contemplation on the following passage:

The authors of the books of Maccabees portray the Lord as punishing the people for ignoring the commands of the Lord. In reality, much of their suffering comes from the greed and desire for power on the part of evil people. The story stresses the need for people to trust God and to pray for the Lord to provide wise and good leaders for their country. It challenges us to reflect on our own need to pray for good leaders.

✠ *What can I learn from this passage?*

## Day 2: Martyrdom of a Mother and Her Seven Sons (6—7)

King Antiochus began a vicious attack against the Temple and the people who were willing to die for the sake of their faith in the Lord. He sent an Athenian senator to force the Jews to reject the laws of God and dedicate the Jewish Temple in Jerusalem and the Samaritan temple on Mount Gerizim to Zeus. They made the sacred courts a place of sexual pleasure with prostitutes and covered the altar with abominable offerings. The king's senator forbade the Jews to follow Jewish laws or openly admit to being a Jew. They had to march wearing wreaths of ivy during the festival of the Greek god, Dionysus.

Jews in other Greek cities had to follow the same laws as those in Judea under pain of death. Two women who had their male infants circumcised were forced to parade about the city with their infants hanging at the breast and then they were thrown down from the city wall. On the Sabbath, many died without retaliating out of respect for the law. The author tells the readers the punishment came to the Jews, not to destroy them, but to correct them. In the end, the Lord will not abandon the people.

A man named Eleazar was being forced to open his mouth to eat pork, but he kept spitting it out. His longtime acquaintances privately encouraged him to pretend to eat the sacrificial meal and instead bring his own provisions to eat. He refused, saying many of the young would think the ninety-year-old Eleazar had accepted an alien religion. Even if he pretended just to gain a brief moment of life, he cannot escape the judgment of the Almighty. The message of Eleazar supports the growing belief in life after death in Jewish writings. He faced his torture and death courageously with joy in his soul, leaving an example of virtue for the young and the whole nation.

Chapter 7 presents a story of courage, faith in God, and hope for a life after death. Seven brothers and their mother were scourged by order of the king to force them to eat pork, which is forbidden by God's law. The first brother, speaking for all of them, declared they were ready to die rather than sin against the laws of their ancestors. The king ordered his tongue to be cut out, his head to be scalped, and his hands and feet cut off while his mother watched. He then ordered the brother to be fried on a heated pan. With the smoke rising from the hot pan, the mother and brothers encouraged each other to die gallantly, quoting Moses, who said God will have compassion on the Lord's servants.

The second brother refused to eat pork, so he also endured the same torture and death as his brother. Before he died he told the king he was depriving them of this life, but the King of the universe will raise them up to live forever because they die faithful to the laws of the Lord.

The third brother immediately put out his tongue when told to do so and stretched out his hands, saying he received them from heaven (God) and for the sake of the laws of the Lord he counts them as nothing, filled with the hope he will receive them again. His willing acceptance of suffering impressed the king and his attendants.

The fourth brother was treated in the same manner, and before he died he declared he had hope the Lord will restore him to life. He states there will be no resurrection to life for the king.

The fifth brother accepted his torture and death bravely, predicting before he died the king would see how the great power of the Lord will torment him and his descendants.

The sixth brother endured the same mistreatment, admitting the nation endured these things due to their sins against God, and the king should not think he will go unpunished for fighting against God.

The mother of the seven brothers encouraged each one in their own language, telling them the Creator of the world who created everything will return breath and life to them because they sacrificed themselves for the sake of the law.

The king attempted to lure the seventh brother with riches and happiness if he would abandon the laws of his ancestors. When this did not work, the king appealed to the mother to save her son's life. After much persuasion, she agreed to save his life, but in a different manner. Recalling for her son all she willingly did to nurture him, she encouraged him not to fear his executioner but to be worthy of his brothers and accept death so she may receive him again with his brothers. Her son suddenly asks the king why he is delaying. Warning the king he will receive punishment, the son prays his death and the death of his brothers will bring an end to the wrath of the Almighty on their nation. The enraged king treated him worse than the others.

The mother was then put to death after her sons.

## *Lectio Divina*

Spend 8 to 10 minutes in silent contemplation of the following passage:

When many of us read about the atrocities endured by those who died for the Lord, we pray we will not have to make such an agonizing choice as the seven sons and their mother did. Whatever is in store for us, we pray we will remain faithful to the end and maintain our hope in life after death.

✠ *What can I learn from this passage?*

---

### Day 3: Victories of Judas and the Purification of the Temple (8—10:9)

The story of Judas Maccabeus continues from 5:27, where Judas Maccabeus withdrew to the wilderness with nine others. The story of Judas in 2 Maccabees follows portions of the exploits of Judas and his brothers found in 1 Maccabees. Judas secretly enters the villages, enlists other faithful Jews, and builds a force of 6,000 men.

Ptolemy of Egypt sent Nicanor with 20,000 men to wipe out the entire Jewish nation. Gorgias, a general, marched with Nicanor. To pay the tribute owed to the Romans, Nicanor intended to sell captured Jews into slavery. Judas encouraged his army to trust in God, who can destroy not only an army but also the whole world. To encourage his men, he referred to a battle when the angels of the Lord routed King Sennacherib and his 185,000 men who were prepared to fight the Israelites (see 2 Kings 19:35–36).

Judas assigned his brothers, Simon, Joseph, and Jonathan, plus Eleazar to lead 1,500 men each. Judas led the first division against Nicanor. They killed more than 9,000 of Nicanor's army, wounded a great many, and sent the rest fleeing.

Judas and his troops rested for the Sabbath, and after the Sabbath divided some of the spoils of the battle to those who were tortured and to widows and orphans. The rest they divided among themselves and their children. Judas defeated the armies of Timothy and Bacchides, killed more than 20,000, and took the spoils. Nicanor, who brought 1,000 slave dealers to buy Jews, was shamed in his defeat.

In chapter 9, Antiochus' forces were routed by the people when they attempted to ransack a Persian temple. When he learned what happened to Nicanor's and Timothy's forces, he became enraged and rushed with his troops to make the Jews pay for their defeat. The Lord God of Israel, however, inflicted him with overwhelming pains in his bowels. In his haste, he fell from a speeding chariot and hurt himself so badly he had to be carried on a litter. In his agony, he gradually changed his attitude toward the Jews and their Temple. He made a number of oaths to the Lord, saying he would become a Jew himself and spread word of the power of God to everyone.

When his sickness grew worse, he named his son, Antiochus, to succeed him. He died an agonizing death (actually around the time of the purification of the Temple, 164 BC). Philip, his foster brother, brought Antiochus' body home and later withdrew to Egypt. The title "foster brother" was often used as an honorary title conferred on a noble by the king and did not necessarily indicate relationship.

At the beginning of chapter 10, Judas Maccabeus took control of the Temple and the city, destroyed the foreigners' altars and shrines and fulfilled the necessary steps for purifying the Temple. They offered sacrifice, burned incense, lit the lamps, and set out the showbread. The feast was celebrated for eight days, known as Hanukkah. The people carried branches and palms and sang hymns of praise. The event is described more at length in 1 Maccabees 4:36–61.

### Lectio Divina

Spend 8 to 10 minutes in silent contemplation of the following passage:

The second Temple in Jerusalem was so sacred to the people they would die to protect it. Judas Maccabeus celebrated the rededication of the Temple as a major feast for Judaism. In the Catholic Church, the church building is also sacred because it is the place where the community gathers to worship God. The place of worship for Judaism and Catholicism is the sacred home of the community and must be treated with respect.

✠ *What can I learn from this passage?*

LESSON 7: THE BOOK OF SECOND MACCABEES

## Day 4: Renewed Persecution (10:10—12)

Antiochus V succeeded his father as king and appointed Lysias commander-in-chief of Coelesyria and Phoenicia. First Maccabees states Lysias raised the young king, who was about nine years old at the time his father died. Lysias governed and waged wars in the young king's name (see 1 Maccabees 6:17).

The Idumeans were harassing the Jews. Judas and his army prayed for the Lord's help and killed 20,000 Idumeans, forcing 9,000 to flee to two towers. Judas left his brothers, Simon and Joseph, along with Zacchaeus, to battle those in the towers. During the siege, some of Simon's men accepted a bribe to allow a number of the Idumeans to escape. When Maccabeus heard of this, he returned, ordered the death of those who took bribes, and seized the towers. He killed more than 20,000 in the two strongholds.

Timothy, already defeated once by the Jews, gathered a large army of foreign troops and cavalry from Asia. Judas' forces, prostrate before the altar, prayed to God for help. They then engaged Timothy's troops a distance from the city. In the midst of the battle, five majestic men from the heavens appeared on golden bridled horses leading the Jews. They surrounded Maccabeus as a shield. They then routed the enemy with their arrows and thunderbolts. A large number of the enemy was killed; Timothy fled to a stronghold known as Gazara.

Maccabeus and his forces fought for four days trying to capture Gazara while the enemy, feeling secure, kept hurling blasphemies at them. On the fifth day, twenty of Maccabeus' young men, angered by the blasphemies, stormed the wall, killing everyone they encountered. Others from Maccabeus' army then followed. They torched the towers, opened the gates for the full force to enter, and killed Timothy, who tried to hide in a cistern.

In chapter 11, the author tells of Lysias' desire to make Jerusalem a Greek city, levy taxes on the Temple, and each year sell the office of high priest to the highest bidder. He attacked a stronghold at Beth-zur. When Maccabeus and his men heard about the attack, they prayed for the Lord's help. As they neared Jerusalem, a horseman in white garments and brandishing gold weapons became their leader. They defeated Lysias' troops, killing or wounding 11,000 foot soldiers and 1,600 cavalry. Lysias fled shamefully.

Lysias, realizing the Jews had God as their ally, negotiated for peace and wrote to the Jews, saying he spoke to the king, who agreed to care for their interests in the future as long as they remained faithful to the king. The king sent a letter to Lysias, telling him to allow the Jews to live in peace and be allowed to follow the customs of their ancestors. In a letter to the Jews, the king declared he would send Menelaus to reassure them of a safe return to their city and follow their dietary laws without any fear of being mistreated. The Romans also sent a letter telling the Jews they agreed with Lysias' peace gestures and asked the Jews to send an envoy to tell them their decision regarding the matters that should be submitted to the king.

In chapter 12, the names of Timothy and Nicanor appear, although an earlier chapter spoke of Timothy's death. The chapter may not be in correct chronological order, or this may be a reference to another person named Timothy.

The people of Joppa, feigning to befriend the Jews, offered them safe passage home by way of the sea. Once out on the water, the people of Joppa drowned at least 200 Jews. When Judas heard about the deception, he attacked Joppa at night, setting the harbor on fire, burning their boats, and killing all who sought refuge there. When he heard the people of Jamnia were also intent on wiping out the Jews, he attacked them at night, burning the harbor and the boats.

About a mile from Jamnia, Arabians numbering about 5,000 foot soldiers and 500 cavalry attacked Judas' troops. Judas' forces defeated them, and they negotiated for peace, promising to supply the army with livestock and offering to serve them in any other way. Knowing they could be useful to him, Judas agreed.

Judas then attacked a well-fortified city called Caspin. Believing they were secure, the people in the stronghold hurled insults at Judas and his men. Judas' troops prayed and were able to slaughter them. The slaughter was so great that a pool nearby, about a quarter-mile wide, appeared to have the blood flowing into it.

Judas' army pursued Timothy as far as a town named Charax, but Timothy already left the city with a force of 125,000 foot soldiers and 2,500 cavalry. He left 10,000 men to defend the city. While Judas led a portion of his troops in pursuit of Timothy, two of Maccabeus' captains captured Charax.

When Timothy realized Judas was close behind him, he sent the women and children on ahead to a well-fortified place called Karnion. At the sight of Judas' army, Timothy's troops panicked and, in their confusion to escape, they unwittingly wounded each other with their sharp swords. Judas killed 30,000 men in the battle.

The army of the two captains who conquered Charax captured Timothy, but Timothy begged for his life, reminding them he had many of their parents and relatives with him, and his forces would kill them. He pledged to free them if the captains did not kill him, so they released him.

Judas continued his pursuit, killing the men in the fortifications along the way. In one town named Scythopolis, Judas learned the people treated the Jews well, so he thanked the inhabitants and urged them to continue to treat the Jewish nation well.

Judas and his army arrived in Jerusalem in time to celebrate the feast of Weeks, which was also called Pentecost. After the feast, they marched against Gorgias, the governor of Idumea. A powerful horseman of Judas' army was able to grab Gorgias by his military cloak and drag him along, intending to capture him alive. An enemy quickly freed Gorgias by cutting off the horseman's arm at the shoulder. During a lull in the battle, Judas prayed for help from the Lord. Suddenly shouting out a battle cry, Judas led his troops against the enemy when they least expected it. They fled before the Jews.

When Judas went to gather the bodies of their fallen comrades for burial, they found under the tunic of each one amulets sacred to the idols of Jamnia, which the soldiers apparently took during the battle in that city. Taking these amulets was forbidden in Deuteronomy 7:25–26, commanding Jews to destroy any images of idols. The author of 2 Maccabees views this abandonment of the Law as the reason for the death of the troops. The surviving troops praise the Lord, the just judge who reveals hidden things.

Judas' troops plead for the forgiveness of the sinful deeds of these men. Their prayer exemplifies a belief in the resurrection of the dead. Taking up a collection among the troops, Judas sent money to Jerusalem for an expiatory sacrifice. If he had not expected a resurrection of the dead, his action would have been unnecessary and foolish. He believed a blessed reward awaited those who died in godliness.

## Lectio Divina

Spend 8 to 10 minutes in silent contemplation of the following passage:

Catholics' belief of praying for the dead is based on 2 Maccabees, which says Judas Maccabeus "made atonement for the dead that they might be absolved from their sin" (12:46). Catholics believe the living as well as the dead belong to the communion of saints, and we can assist each other by our prayers.

✠ *What can I learn from this passage?*

_____

## Day 5: Nicanor's Death (13—15)

Judas heard Antiochus Eupator was invading Judea with a Greek force of 110,000 foot soldiers, 5,300 cavalry, twenty-two elephants, and 300 armed chariots. Lysias and Menelaus marched with them. Menelaus was hoping for a high office from the king, but Lysias revealed to the king the trouble caused by Menelaus. The king ordered Menelaus to be thrown off a seventy-five foot tower into smoldering ashes. Since Menelaus committed so many crimes against the altar with fire and ashes, the author of 2 Maccabees views this as a suitable punishment for such a wicked villain.

At Judas' urging, the people prayed continuously for God's help, weeping, fasting, and prostrating themselves before the Lord for three days. Taking counsel with the elders, Judas decided to march out and meet the Greek army before they could invade the city. He encouraged the people to fight to the death for the Law, the Temple, the city, the country, and the government. He camped a short distance from the enemy. At night, Judas invaded the king's camp with specially picked brave warriors, killing 2,000. He stabbed the lead elephant and its rider and withdrew victorious as dawn was breaking.

The king attempted to march against Beth-zur, but he was driven back. Judas sent supplies to the men inside the city. The king negotiated peace with the people of Beth-zur and went to fight against Judas, who defeated him.

The king learned about a rebellion led by Philip, whom the king left at Antioch in charge of the government. In his haste to return home, he negotiated with the Jews, submitting to their terms and swearing to observe all their rights. He then offered sacrifice, honored the sanctuary, gave a generous donation, appointed a governor for the territory, and departed. When he came to Ptolemais, the angry populace wanted to reject the treaty he made with Judas, but Lysias convinced them to accept it. The king and Lysias returned to Antioch.

In chapter 14, Demetrius, the son of Seleucus, occupied the country and ordered the king and Lysias killed. A wicked former high priest named Alcimus presented Demetrius with a gold crown, a palm branch, and some olive branches from the Temple. He said nothing on that occasion but later told the king a group called the Hasideans, led by Judas Maccabeus, were warmongers who kept the kingdom from attaining peace. First Maccabees portrayed the Hasideans as a party separate from the Maccabees (see 1 Maccabees 2:42 and 7:12–17). He reported peace in the kingdom was impossible as long as Judas lived. The Friends of the king who were also hostile to Judas added to Alcimus' condemnation of Judas.

King Demetrius chose Nicanor, who was in charge of the elephants and governor of Judea, to kill Judas, disperse his followers, and establish Alcimus as high priest. When the Gentiles, who fled from Judea because of Judas, heard about Nicanor, they rallied behind him, thinking the destruction of the Jews would lead to their prosperity. When the Jews heard Nicanor was coming, they sprinkled themselves with earth and prayed to God.

Hearing about the valor and courage of Judas and his men, Nicanor sent three men to exchange pledges of friendship with Judas. They set a date when the leaders would meet by themselves. Fearing the enemy might be plotting against him, Judas placed his men in strategic positions where they could quickly defend him. The conference was held in peace.

Nicanor remained in Jerusalem where he disbanded the throngs of people around him and always kept Judas in his company, feeling affection for him. He urged Judas to marry, have children, and settle down, which is what he did.

When Alcimus saw the favor existing between Nicanor and Judas, he reported to the king that Nicanor was plotting against him, planning to appoint Judas as his successor. The furious king wrote a letter to Nicanor, informing him he was displeased with the treaty and ordering him to send Maccabeus to Antioch as a prisoner. Although Nicanor became deeply troubled by the order to annul the agreement and arrest Judas, who had done no wrong, he watched for an opportunity to fulfill the king's order. When he began to treat Judas more harshly and with greater rudeness, Judas concluded the harshness was not a good sign, so he gathered some of his men and went into hiding.

When Nicanor realized Judas had gone into hiding, he went to the Temple and threatened the priests, demanding them to hand Judas over to him. Stretching out his right arm toward the Temple and swearing an oath, he told them he would level the shrine of God to the ground, tear down the altar, and erect a shrine to Dionysus if they did not hand Judas over to him. Under oath, the priest said they did not know where Judas was hiding. After Nicanor left, the priests prayed the Lord of all holiness would preserve forever the Temple which was recently purified.

A man named Razis, one of the elders in Jerusalem, was called the father of the Jews because of his favorable treatment of them. Nicanor, believing he could wound the Jews deeply by arresting Razis, sent more than 500 soldiers for him. To avoid such a humiliating arrest, Razis tried to stab himself with his sword but failed. In a second attempt to take his own life, he jumped off the top wall of his stronghold, but he did not die. Finally, bleeding and weak, he tore out his insides and hurled them into the crowd, praying the Lord would give these back to him again.

In chapter 15, Nicanor, learning Judas and his companions were in Samaria, believed he could safely attack on the Sabbath. When the Jews with Nicanor declared the living Lord commanded the observance of the Sabbath day, Nicanor proclaimed himself the ruler on earth and commanded them to arm themselves and fulfill the king's wish. Nicanor was determined to be victorious over Judas, but Judas reminded his men how the Lord helped them in the past and to expect a victory now.

Judas encouraged them with words from the Law and the prophets. He lifted their spirits by relating a dream he had that was more like a waking vision. He saw Onias, the saintly high priest, praying with arms outstretched for the whole Jewish community. Another man appeared, distinguished by his white hair, whom Onias introduced as Jeremiah. Jeremiah presented a golden sword to Judas, telling him to accept the sword as a gift from God, for it will shatter his enemies.

Having been inspired by Judas' words, his troops were prepared to charge gallantly into hand-to-hand combat with the enemy. The concern of the men for the protection of the sanctuary and Temple was greater than their concern for their families. When Judas witnessed the power of the enemy forces, he spread out his hands toward heaven, knowing it was not weapons but the Lord who brought victory to those who deserve it. He prayed the Lord would send angels to help them as the Lord did in the days of Hezekiah, when the Lord slew 185,000 men of King Sennacherib (see 2 Kings 19:35–36). In the battle, the Jews killed 35,000 and celebrated God's powerful help. They celebrated even more when they discovered Nicanor's body among the dead.

Judas ordered Nicanor's head and his right arm up to the shoulder severed from his body. The severing of Nicanor's right arm was in retaliation for his gesture of stretching his arm toward the Temple and swearing he would tear it down if the priests did not reveal Judas' hiding place. Judas brought Nicanor's head and right arm to Jerusalem. Assembling all the people and priests, he showed them Nicanor's head and the right arm Nicanor boastfully stretched out against them. Nicanor spoke arrogantly with his tongue, declaring at one time he was the ruler on earth. Judas cut out Nicanor's tongue and fed it to the birds.

All the people praised the Lord for protecting the sacred sanctuary. As a certain sign of the help the Lord provides for the people, Judas suspended Nicanor's head and arm on the wall of the citadel.

In an epilogue, the author, declaring the city remained in the possession of the Hebrews from that day forward, brings his story to an end. He ends by saying, "...a skillfully composed story delights the ears of those who read the work" (15:39).

## *Lectio Divina*

Spend 8 to 10 minutes in silent contemplation of the following passage:

When Nicanor agreed to live in peace with Judas Maccabeus and suggested he marry and raise a family, Judas immediately settled into family life. The occasion offers an insight into Judas' plight. He wanted to live an ordinary life, faithful to the covenant and raising a family, but his zeal for the Temple and the people of the nation forced him to fight against those who would abuse or destroy the sacred Temple and the people of his nation. Throughout history, good people often had to defend other people by fighting for them. In the midst of all his battles, Judas prayed for help from the Lord. He was a man of deep faith.

✠ *What can I learn from this passage?*

## *Review Questions*

1. What does 2 Maccabees say about Onias?
2. How did the high priests in 2 Maccabees influence the life of the people?
3. What do we learn from the story of Eleazar and the story of the seven sons?
4. Why is the purification of the Temple so important?

# About the Author

**William A. Anderson, DMin, PhD,** is a presbyter of the diocese of Wheeling-Charleston, West Virginia. A director of retreats and parish missions, professor, catechist, spiritual director, and a former pastor, he has written extensively on pastoral, spiritual, and religious subjects. Father Anderson earned his doctor of ministry degree from St. Mary's Seminary & University in Baltimore and his doctorate in sacred theology from Duquesne University in Pittsburgh.

## Liguori Catholic Bible Study Series

**Introduction to the Bible:** *Overview, Historical Context, and Cultural Perspectives* • 821196

### OLD TESTAMENT

**Pentateuch I:** *Creation and Covenant* (Genesis and Exodus) • 821318

**Pentateuch II:** *Shaping the Israelite Community*
(Leviticus, Numbers, and Deuteronomy) • 821325

**Historical Books I:** *Joshua, Judges, Ruth, 1 and 2 Samuel* • 821332

**Historical Books II:** *1 and 2 Kings, 1 and 2 Chronicles, Ezra, Nehemiah* • 821349

**Biblical Novellas:** *Tobit, Judith, Esther, 1 and 2 Maccabees* • 821387

**Wisdom Books:** *Job, Psalms, Proverbs, Ecclesiastes, Song of Songs,*
*Wisdom, Sirach (Ben Sira)* • 821394

**Prophets I:** *Isaiah, Jeremiah, Lamentations, Baruch* • 821356

**Prophets II:** *Ezekiel and Daniel* • 821363

**Prophets III:** *Hosea, Joel, Amos, Obadiah, Jonah, Micah, Nahum, Habakkuk,*
*Zephaniah, Haggai, Zechariah, Malachi* • 821370

### NEW TESTAMENT

**The Gospel of Matthew:** *Proclaiming the Ministry of Jesus* • 821202

**The Gospel of Mark:** *Revealing the Mystery of Jesus* • 821219

**The Gospel of Luke:** *Salvation for All Humanity* • 821226

**The Gospel of John:** *The Word Became Flesh* • 821233

**The Acts of the Apostles:** *Good News for All People* • 821240

**Letters to the Romans and Galatians:** *Reconciling the Old and New Covenants* • 821257

**Letters to the Corinthians:** *Gifts of the Holy Spirit* • 821264

**Paul's Early and Prison Letters:** *1 and 2 Thessalonians, Philippians, Colossians,*
*Ephesians, Philemon* • 821271

**Pastoral Letters and The Letter to the Hebrews:** *1 and 2 Timothy, Titus, Hebrews* • 821288

**Universal Letters:** *James, 1 and 2 Peter, 1, 2, and 3 John, Jude* • 821295

**The Book of Revelation:** *Hope in the Midst of Persecution* • 821301

*To order, visit your local bookstore, call 800-325-9521, or visit us at liguori.org.*

CPSIA information can be obtained at www.ICGtesting.com
Printed in the USA
LVOW10s1920051214

417397LV00006B/7/P

9 780764 821387